Vancouver

REEL Vancouver

An INSIDER'S Guide

Ken MacIntyre

Whitecap Books
Vancouver/Toronto

Edited by Carolyn Bateman
Proofread by Elizabeth McLean
Cover design by Warren Clark
Cover photograph by Ryan McNair
Interior design and typesetting by Margaret Ng
Photo Credits: Trevor Hodgson, pages 6, 7, 12, 23, 24, 31, 32, 34, 40, 43, 45, 50, 53, 56, 59, 60, 62, 64, 72, 90, 97, 103, 113, 118, 132. Ken MacIntyre, pages 15, 18, 19, 22, 27, 36, 37, 38, 47, 51, 55, 67, 68, 69, 70, 71, 74, 80, 89, 92, 94, 105. Claus P. Wagenblast, pages 65, 79. Joseph Lederer page 9. Michael Lavine/Fox page 76.

Printed and bound in Canada.

Canadian Cataloguing in Publication Data
MacIntyre, Ken
Reel Vancouver

Includes bibliographical references and index.
ISBN 1-55110-506-3

1. Motion picture industry—British Columbia—Vancouver Metropolitan Area. 2. Television broadcasting—British Columbia—Vancouver Metropolitan Area. I. Title.

PN1993.5.C22V35 1996 384'.8'0971133 C96-910364-6

CONTENTS

INTRODUCTION

This is a guidebook that was born out of frustration. Not the kind of frustration inherent in researching and assembling a book of this kind, but a frustration that comes from circling a congested city block that yields no parking spaces. A feeling Vancouverites sympathize with.

Many of us have driven downtown unable to find a vacant spot or been rerouted in a direction we hadn't anticipated. We curse at the big white trucks that seem to stretch for blocks and are peevishly indignant when asked by orange-vested flunkies to "be quiet." Yet we are undeniably fascinated with the films and TV shows shot on our city's streets.

On one particular occasion I was driving along Smithe looking for that ever elusive parking space when I hung a right on Robson. In front of the Vancouver Art Gallery, dozens of onlookers jammed the sidewalks, straining for a glimpse of the celebrity-du-jour. Was it Mel Gibson? Sly Stallone? Sharon Stone?

I had deposited myself in the middle of a major "on location" production . . . great. Frustration predictably turned to wonder, then excitement. *This is* Hollywood North after all.

Was that *Star Trek's* Leonard Nimoy?!

It was. And the shoot turned out to be an episode of the syndicated television series *The Outer Limits*. Imagine, Mr. Spock, right here in Vancouver.

This was the event that sparked the genesis of *Reel Vancouver*. It's an idea whose time had definitely come, and one, I'm glad to say, that has given me a greater appreciation for the city's filmmaking stature. Long before I embarked on this undertaking, however, the seed of my obsession had already been planted.

Although no streets or thoroughfares bear his name, Burnaby native Michael J. Fox does have a theatre named after him. It's in Burnaby South Secondary (5455 Rumble Street) where he attended high school. Before becoming a household name with starring roles in the TV series *Family Ties* and the *Back to the Future* film trilogy, he starred in the Vancouver-made CBC series called *Leo and Me*, which the CBC later tried to sell internationally. There were no takers.

I was first hooked on the movies when my dad took me to see Charlie Chaplin's *Modern Times* at the old Coronet Theatre when I was eight years old, and like many Vancouverites, my love of motion pictures has flourished with the growth of our own film industry. Twenty-odd years later, I am now fortunate enough to work in this industry, which allows me to indulge my obsession while appearing to hold down a bonafide job.

Moviemaking has been happening here since the turn of the century. Film pioneer Thomas Edison shot some of the province's earliest footage in 1900, and returned several years later to produce promotional films for the CPR. Many Hollywood stars appeared in B.C.-made movies in the years that followed, including Rita Hayworth, Lillian Gish, Peter Lawford, and Shelley Winters. A lot of these films provided the lush exterior backdrops needed to augment footage filmed in Hollywood.

In the 1960s and 1970s, more realism entered into motion pictures, and influential filmmakers such as Robert Altman and Mike Nichols chose to shoot entire movies on location in and around Vancouver as an alternative to Hollywood's restrictive sound stages. By the 1980s the cheap Canadian dollar had lured the big studios here as well. Blockbuster movies such as *Look Who's Talking*, *Rocky IV*, and *Stakeout* confirmed the city's burgeoning reputation as a first-class production centre, and the nineties have seen Vancouver become the industry's second largest producer of episodic television.

For some time, then, our city has been bristling with actors and big-budget productions, a sight seldom seen outside Los Angeles or New York. Unlike the American tradition of big walls and closed sets though, filmmaking in Vancouver can be people-friendly. If you know where you're going, locals and tourists alike can "stumble" onto a dozen different productions in a day. It's possible to walk from Gastown to Montana, from Stanley Park to San Francisco, from the West End to *The Outer Limits*, without ever leaving the city.

Home of the third largest production centre in North America, Vancouver is *real*. You can watch a feature film or a network television show being shot right across your street. You can even eat at the same restaurant and enjoy movies at the same cinema as famous celebrities you'd never catch a glimpse of while vacationing in Los Angeles.

With this in mind, I set out to explore the city's most popular and frequently filmed landmarks and the roles they've played in some of Hollywood's biggest movies and TV shows.

Before joining the TV series *Beverly Hills 90210*, Vancouver's Jason Priestly played dozens of roles in local productions, most notably as one of Corey Haim's pals in the locally filmed sci-fi thriller *Watchers*. It was at the suspension bridge in the Capilano River Regional Park that Priestly's character was chased and killed by the film's crazed monster.

Between watching more than three hundred hours of made-in-Vancouver productions, and driving endlessly around the city's streets and back alleys, I discovered that the film industry here is far more pervasive than I'd thought. I personally stumbled onto *seven* different location shoots in a single afternoon and spotted twice as many celebrities in a week. Shop owners and restaurateurs bragged to me about how many times their businesses had been seen on-screen, and behind-the-scenes set visits resulted in some juicy film facts, which I've catalogued in the boxed "factoids."

As well as this extensive location-by-location film guide to Vancouver's "Studio Zone," I've also included step-by-step instructions on how to gracefully crash a location shoot. Star-gazing is made more accessible with tips on celebrity hot spots. Comprehensive location listings from the critically acclaimed *X-Files* TV series (of which I'm a big fan) are provided, as well as a B.C. filmography dating all the way back to the 1900s that reveals many surprises about who and what has been shot in Hollywood North.

After an exhilarating year spent researching this guide, my once familiar city has become one giant movie set. I can't walk down the street without pointing out locations. The Marine Building is no longer just an office tower since Jean-Claude Van Damme fell from its top storey in *Timecop*. Gastown isn't just an historic tourist destination. Brad Pitt, Julia Ormond, and Aidan Quinn lived their turn-of-the-century lives there in *Legends of the Fall*. And I don't think of Grouse Mountain as a place to ski any more; it's now the spot from which Gillian Anderson was abducted by "aliens" in *The X-Files*.

Yes, it was an interesting year, one I won't remember for its frustrations but rather for the sense of excitement and fascination generated by Vancouver and its film industry. Perhaps *Reel Vancouver* will also instill in you this same fascination with the film world. Whether you decide to lie back on your couch and watch a made-in-B.C. flick or head out into Hollywood's biggest backlot with *Reel Vancouver* in your hand, you may never look at this city the same way again. I know I won't.

> Shortly after filming began on the action picture *Rumble in the Bronx*, Jackie Chan thought about changing the film's name to *Rumble in Vancouver* because the New York borough was too difficult to duplicate. The original title stuck though because the set dressers had already covered the city in Bronx-like graffiti.

SO YOU WANT TO CRASH A LOCATION SHOOT?

In a single year nearly a hundred productions will hit the streets of Vancouver. For many people this is an irresistible situation: a chance to share in the sheer thrill of movie-making. It is quite possible to watch a scene unfold right in front of your eyes, meet the actors, or actually participate in a big-budget production. All you have to do is track down a film shoot, which needn't be an intimidating or mystifying endeavour. In fact, in Vancouver it can be as easy as tracking down a good cup of caffe latte.

But where do you begin?

1. Timing is everything: Although Vancouver streets are always busy with location filming (with the exception of two weeks during the Christmas season), the busiest time of year is usually from the end of July to the end of October. This is when all the television series that are gearing up for their fall seasons join the rest of the productions already in progress.

2. Hot tips: The B.C. Film Commission posts a weekly "hot sheet" listing all the feature films, made-for-TV movies, and television series currently in production. This list is available at the B.C. Film Commission office (601 West Cordova Street), Monday to Friday, 8:30 A.M.–4:30 P.M., or by phoning their hot-line at 604-660-3569.

3. Going public: Production companies will not reveal the location where a film is scheduled to shoot, unless of course it's in a public gathering place where lots of people are expected to be anyway (like a shopping centre). And even then, most companies feel onlookers will impede their crews' shooting schedule. Direct phone calls to the production companies are usually fruitless and are discouraged, but

Jodie Foster won her first Academy Award for her performance in the Vancouver-filmed *Reckless Endangerment.* If that doesn't ring a bell it's because the release title was later changed to *The Accused.*

there are more devious methods you can resort to.

4. Doing your homework: Vancouver's *The Province* newspaper has a showbiz columnist who sometimes divulges information about what's shooting where. Lynne McNamara's "The Insider" column runs every Friday and is a great place to find out about celebrities in town.

Other Vancouver media outlets that cover the local showbiz buzz include CFOX 99.3 FM, weekdays at 6:00 P.M., and BCTV's Early News on Mondays at 5:20 P.M. Every Thursday morning, from 6:00 to 9:00, Z95.3 FM takes listeners' phone calls in a segment called "Star Spy Thursday," and Lynne McNamara also covers the local entertainment industry daily on CKWX News 1130.

5. Knowing the signs: To track down a shoot, keep an eye out for unusual traffic and street signs. Many companies will post fluorescent-coloured arrows to help guide their crews to locations. These signs are usually little more than half a metre wide and hold an abbreviated version of the production's name (i.e., "*The Commish*" would become "*Com*" or "*The X-Files*" might be "*X-F*"). You can use these signs to help guide *yourself* to the same locations. Sometimes even "temporary no parking" signs can provide clues to a cast and crew's impending arrival. Then again, they could simply mean that city workers will be tearing up the street.

Production company signs, such as this one from the film *Alaska,* can help you find a shoot.

6. Follow that truck: If you see a conspicuous cavalcade of big white trucks and trailers, especially ones with the words "mobile dressing

Big white trucks are a sure sign that the "circus" is in town.

rooms" or "location caterers" written on their sides, this is a definite indication that the "circus," or location shoot, is nearby. These "honey-wagons" usually occupy entire street blocks and parking lots, so they're not exactly difficult to spot. If you encounter such vehicles in transit, chances are they're either going to or coming from a shoot.

7. Talking to strangers: If you're walking down the street and notice that something doesn't seem quite right, such as a *USA Today* newspaper box where it shouldn't be, or a snow-covered hedge in July, chances are the set dressers from a film shoot have been around. If you haven't already noticed the telltale signs described in steps 5 and 6, speak with local business people or residents. This can be a good way of finding out what's going on. Did the shoot just wrap, is the crew about to set up, or are they coming back tomorrow?

8. Letter of intent: Filming notification letters are usually distributed to residences and businesses a few days before a production is scheduled to shoot. These inform locals of any temporary disruptions that may occur in a specified area (such as the blowing up of a neighbouring building or a plane landing on the street). Sometimes these notices can be found posted in apartment building lobbies and store windows, in which case you'll have plenty of time to plan your visit.

Oops! Take 1: During the filming of *Rocky IV*, more than five hundred take-out boxes of KFC were brought in to feed hundreds of extras. The order was piled onto outdoor tables at Exhibition Park, but they ended up sitting in the sun so long the city health inspector was forced to throw them all in the garbage.

9. Extra, extra: Becoming an "extra" can be the most accessible way to experience the behind-the-scenes excitement of being on-set. As an extra you help provide the production with a controllable background to the main action of the film. Even with limited time and without an agent, there are plenty of ways to get involved. Sometimes productions require large crowd scenes, in which case the call goes out via radio announcements and newspaper listings. Also, watch for open casting-call notices printed in regional newspapers or posted in community centres. There *are* several talent agencies who specialize in extra casting for those with the time to pursue a more active role in the film industry. Check out *The Georgia Straight*'s callboard column or pick up a copy of the *Reel West Digest* for comprehensive listings.

10. You've arrived: Once you've arrived at a location shoot, watch for the production assistants, or PAs. They can usually be spotted wearing a coloured vest and carrying a walkie-talkie. It's the PA's job to direct traffic, answer questions, and instruct onlookers where to stand.

11. Don't make a move: While on location, remember that the crew and actors are doing a job, and as such should not be interrupted. If the opportunity to speak with one of the film's stars arises, however, be polite and chances are you could come away with a photo or an autograph.

12. The accidental spectator: Some location managers welcome the public to stay and watch. It not only gives them a chance to expose people to a sometimes elusive and bewildering industry, it also helps create a "film smart" and "film friendly" community in which to work.

VANCOUVER "STUDIO ZONE" LOCATIONS

Scores of frequently filmed landmarks and locales from around this region have been seen in TV series, feature films, made-for-TV movies, music videos, and commercials. It would be impossible to list them all so we've concentrated on the most popular and visible locations.

Only notable TV shows and movies are included within each listing, while made-for-TV movies have, for the most part, been omitted simply because of their fleeting nature.

This section has been arranged geographically. Individual locations have then been listed alphabetically.

Mel Gibson and Goldie Hawn scramble across the top of Vancouver's Metropolitan Hotel (645 Howe Street) in the action movie *Bird on a Wire*.

B.C. Place Stadium

Features: *Bingo, Immediate Family, Timecop*
TV Series: *Death of the Incredible Hulk, Highlander, The Outer Limits, Sliders, 21 Jumpstreet, The X-Files*

Home to the B.C. Lions football team and the B.C. Sports Hall of Fame and Museum (604-687-5520), "the dome" is the largest air-supported domed stadium in the world. Its sixty-thousand-seat capacity and vast space also make it ideal for major events like trade shows and rock concerts.

You'll find it next to the north end of the Cambie Street Bridge, downtown. In fact, B.C. Place Stadium is difficult to miss. No matter how hard Hollywood tries to hide it, it keeps popping up in the most unexpected films. Watch for it in *Stakeout, Rumble in the Bronx, Man of the House,* and *The NeverEnding Story,* among others.

In the science-fiction movie *Timecop,* B.C. Place Stadium doubled as the interior of the futuristic T.E.C. Complex in Washington, D.C. It was here that Jean-Claude Van Damme worked as part of a time-travel enforcement agency.

On occasion, the dome has also played an actual football stadium. It stood in as Seattle's King Dome in the drama *Immediate Family,* and was featured in the lost-dog comedy *Bingo.*

Canada Harbour Place

Features: *The Hunted, NeverEnding Story 2, Shoot to Kill, Virtual Assassins*
TV Series: *Cobra, Highlander, MacGyver, The Marshal, 21 Jumpstreet*

Canada Harbour Place (999 Canada Place) was built to house the country's national pavilion during Expo 86 and is now home to the Vancouver Trade and Convention Centre, the CN IMAX Theatre, the Prow Restaurant, a cruise ship terminal, and the luxurious Pan Pacific Hotel. It has since become one of the city's most striking landmarks characterized by its unique Teflon-coated white sails.

Though its exterior is architecturally distinct and therefore very "location specific," the interior of Canada Place has been used by film companies needing large and diverse indoor spaces. The convention centre's concourse level can pass for a train station or an airport terminal simply by installing video monitors and adding sound effects, while the hotel and restaurants get a lot of mileage doubling as . . . hotels and restaurants.

In the thriller *Shoot to Kill,* Sidney Poitier and Tom Berenger chased a kidnapper through the streets of Vancouver and managed to wind up at a BC Ferries terminal next to Canada Place. The terminal in question is actually located in Tsawwassen, but in the movies, of course, anything is possible.

> Director Michael Cimino's action film *Year of the Dragon* is noteworthy not only for its use of local colour, but also for its screenplay, which was written by Oliver Stone.

In the action film *The Hunted,* Christopher Lambert escaped the evil Mikado gang by catching a Japanese bullet train at the Nagoya train station. This scene took place on the convention centre's concourse level.

Gastown

Features: *Another Stakeout, Bird on a Wire, The Changeling, Cold Front, Flinch, The Hitman, Intersection, Legends of the Fall, Look Who's Talking, Look Who's Talking Too, Man of the House, Mystery Date, The NeverEnding Story 1 and 2, North of Pittsburgh, Rumble in the Bronx, Run, Russian Roulette, Shoot to Kill, Short Time, Stay Tuned, Unforgettable*
TV Series: *The Adventures of Beans Baxter, The Beachcombers, Birdland, Booker, The Commish, Constable Constable, Danger Bay, Death of the Incredible Hulk, Doctor Who, Highlander, Jack's Place, MacGyver, Madison, Neon Rider, Nightmare Cafe, Poltergeist: The Legacy, Sliders, Strange Luck, Traps, Trial of the Incredible Hulk, 21 Jumpstreet, Unsub, Wiseguy, The X-Files*

Bordered by Richards and Main Streets, Cordova and the waterfront, this once rough-and-tumble logging community sprang to life around Gassy Jack's saloon in the late 1860s. Affectionately referred to as "the birthplace of Vancouver," the Gastown heritage zone is now an eccentric mix of tourist boutiques and funky fashion outlets sharing street space with designer lofts and skid row areas. It also boasts the only steam-operated clock in the world.

Richard Gere and Lolita Davidovich strolled down historic Water Street on their way to real-life Vancouver architect Arthur Erickson's

Gastown's Water Street is one of the busiest locations in Vancouver.

Gastown offices in the opening scenes of the drama *Intersection*.

In the sweeping historical epic *Legends of the Fall*, Alexander Street, between Carrall and Columbia, was displayed in all its original glory after TriStar Pictures spent $1.2 million transforming the once seedy spot into the bustling turn-of-the-century Montana town of Helena, home to Aidan Quinn, Julia Ormond, and Brad Pitt.

A Cordova Street parking lot was the site of the New Wa Ha Supermarket where Jackie Chan rumbled with assorted hoods and mobsters in the action flick *Rumble in the Bronx*. The lot, which still bears some of the set's graffiti, is located on Cordova's 100 block across from the old Woodward's Building Parkade, which was also featured in the film.

Gastown's distinctive Europe Hotel has also been featured onscreen many times: as the bookstore Jonathan Brandis frequented in *The NeverEnding Story 2* and as the historical society office where George C. Scott found information on the haunted house he'd purchased, in *The Changeling*.

The TV series *Highlander* has filmed several Gastown locations for recurring star turns. Joe's Bookstore can be found at Maple Tree Square, Adrian Paul's dojo is at the corner of Water and Cambie Streets behind the steam clock, and Blood Alley is the site of the Noel and MacLeod Antique Shoppe.

The Dominion Hotel (210 Abbott Street) stands in for San Francisco's Dominion Hotel on the science-fiction television series *Sliders*.

Victory Square Park, at the corner of West Hastings and Cambie Streets near Gastown, is another often employed location. Though it was a major public gathering place in the early 1900s, today it's frequented by the area's homeless, drawing crowds only on Remembrance Day or when a film crew visits. In the comedy *Another Stakeout,* Richard Dreyfuss and Emilio Estevez chased a criminal through Victory Square and into a Gastown alley during one of the opening scenes.

During the 1930s, Hollywood companies descended upon Victoria to make "quota quickie" films. These movies qualified as British productions and could be sold to the protectionist U.K. market for a fast buck. After the quota system was revised in 1938, excluding movies made in the dominions, B.C.'s feature film industry seemed to dry up.

Harbour Centre Tower

Features: *Another Stakeout, Bad Company, Bird on a Wire, Man of the House, Mortal Sins, Virtual Assassins*
TV Series: *Booker, Diagnosis Murder, Madison, Mantis, The Sentinel, Street Justice, Trial of the Incredible Hulk*

Located at the edge of Gastown on the corner of Seymour and West Hastings Streets, Harbour Centre's tower is one of the most "location-specific" sights in Vancouver. The distinctive tower was originally built as part of a business and shopping complex in the early 1970s, and is now also home to Simon Fraser University's downtown annex. The popular tourist spot The Lookout! (604-689-0421), perched atop the building, provides a unique vantage point for spectacular city, ocean, and mountain views.

In the opening scenes of the science-fiction thriller *Virtual Assassins,* which starred Michael Dudikoff, special effects helped make the Harbour Centre Tower look like part of a space-age city.

Hotel Vancouver

Features: *Bad Company, Double Cross, Russian Roulette, Timecop*
TV Series: *The Commish, Highlander, MacGyver, Mantis, The Marshal, Profit, Robin's Hoods, The X-Files*

Before playing a cop in movies such as *Mad Dog and Glory* and *Jade*, and on television in *NYPD Blue*, David Caruso played a cop (a deputy sheriff to be exact) who was beaten up by Sylvester Stallone in the made-in-B.C. film *First Blood*.

The Hotel Vancouver (900 West Georgia Street) was built by the Canadian Northern Railway in 1928 and remained unfinished during the Great Depression until King George VI took the throne in 1939. Unique among today's modern hotels, "the Vancouver" exhibits a seldom seen grandeur characterized by its distinctive green roof and elegant lobby.

In its heyday, Dal Richards and his Big Band packed guests into the hotel's Roof Restaurant (604-684-3131) while many renowned entertainers made it their hotel of choice. The 1941 Oscar-winning feature *The 49th Parallel* even shot scenes on the fourteenth-floor terrace but they were subsequently left on the cutting-room floor.

Today, the Hotel Vancouver still entertains many stars, a lot of whom stay here during the Vancouver International Film Festival every October.

The climax to the 1975 thriller *Russian Roulette* unfolded on the hotel's roof as George Segal fired upon an unsuspecting helicopter. Perhaps more interesting, though, is to watch the film now and see how Vancouver's skyline has changed in the intervening years.

The Marine Building

Features: *Crying Freeman, Look Who's Talking Too, The Road Home, Stay Tuned, Timecop*
TV Series: *The Hat Squad, The Odyssey, Trial of the Incredible Hulk, The X-Files*

This striking example of Art Deco architecture at 355 Burrard Street was erected as an office tower in 1929. Today, it still functions as an office building but also stands as a monument to the city's past. You get a stunning view of the Marine Building from The Lookout! at Harbour Centre Tower.

In fact, the Harbour Centre Tower can actually be seen reflected in the glass of the Marine Building during a scene from the science-fiction film *Timecop*. Look for it while Jason Schombing and Jean-Claude Van Damme are falling from the building's top storey window.

Its spectacular lobby entrance was also featured in *Timecop* as a Wall Street brokerage house.

And the Marine Building has ably played other locales: a Four Seasons Hotel in the drama *Crying Freeman*, a New York City medical building in the comedy *Look Who's Talking Too*, and the law offices where Rex Smith defended Bill Bixby in the TV movie *Trial of the Incredible Hulk*.

The Marine Building's striking Art Deco architecture lends itself well to the movies.

Nightclubs

Features: *Hideaway, Leaving Normal, Mystery Date, Roxanne, Rumble in the Bronx, Short Time, Star 80, Whale Music*
TV Series: *Booker, The Commish, Madison, Neon Rider, Once a Thief, 21 Jumpstreet, Wiseguy, The X-Files*

From rhythm and blues to acid jazz, to hard-core grunge and high-energy dance, downtown Vancouver offers a great mix of bars and clubs for every taste. The Starfish Room on Homer Street and the Railway Club on Dunsmuir Street feature live alternative bands, while The Yale Hotel on Granville Street has some of the best R&B in the city. For dance music, gay clubs such as The Odyssey on Howe Street and Celebrities on Davie Street are good bets, and Mars on Richards Street caters to a young, hip, groovy set.

While most of these Vancouver nightclubs have occasionally helped film crews, there are a few night spots that have been called on repeatedly by the movie industry.

Richards on Richards, an upscale "meet market" found, surprisingly enough, on Richards Street, doubled as the 279 Club in the comedy *Roxanne*. Most movie buffs will hardly forget how Steve Martin listed twenty insults about his big nose while Daryl Hannah, Shelley Duvall, and a bar full of Vancouver extras looked on. In the road movie *Leaving Normal*, Meg Tilly and Christine Lahti watched as Patrika Darbo tried fruitlessly to get someone to dance with her.

Oops! Take 2: In 1987, during filming of an early episode of the TV series *Wise Guy*, the show's effects team actually blew up a glass elevator on the outside of Vancouver's Hyatt Hotel. The lift's "earthquake failsafe" was activated, preventing it from coming down fast enough for the fire to be extinguished. Many guests were said to have run screaming from their rooms believing the building was on fire.

Graceland, also on Richards Street, is a large warehouselike dance club that's popular for its house music. In the comedy *Mystery Date*, Ethan Hawke came looking for his brother here but instead found a dead body!

The dance club Twilight Zone, in historic Gastown, was featured in the science-fiction thriller *Hideaway*, where Alicia Silverstone was nearly seduced by psychotic killer Jeremy Sisto.

Vancouver's premiere strip club is the Penthouse on Seymour Street. Here, Eric Roberts, playing the boyfriend of murdered actress Dorothy Stratten in the Bob Fosse-directed docudrama *Star 80*, hustled anything that moved. During *Star 80*'s location filming someone was overheard asking, "Who is Eric Roberts anyway?" A crew member replied, "I dunno, but he's gonna be big!" Eric's still waiting, but sister Julia is one of the highest paid actresses in Hollywood.

In the drama *Whale Music*, Maury Chaykin walked across the Second Narrows Bridge and miraculously wound up in front of the Penthouse where he wandered in looking for Cyndy Preston. This being the movies, a brawl naturally ensued.

The Penthouse also doubled as a biker bar in the John Woo-directed television movie, *Once a Thief*.

The Orpheum Theatre

Features: *Bliss, The Changeling, Harmony Cats, Knight Moves, Look Who's Talking Too, Power of Attorney, Underworld*
TV Series: *Highlander, Robin's Hoods, The Sentinel, Sliders, The X-Files*

Vancouver's Orpheum Theatre (604-665-3050) was built by the Chicago Orpheum Vaudeville Company in 1927 and was once the largest theatre of its kind in Canada. It was later sold to Famous Players where such "event" motion pictures as *Gone with the Wind* and

The Godfather were exhibited in all their original splendour. In the mid seventies, the building was designated a heritage site and today the Vancouver Symphony Orchestra calls the Orpheum home. Much of Vancouver's show-biz history is housed within the walls of the theatre, and tours are given on a regular basis.

Before gaining international acclaim for hits like *The Crying Game* and *Interview with the Vampire,* Neil Jordan cut his teeth directing movies such as the locally filmed comedy *We're No Angels.*

In the Seattle-based horror film *The Changeling,* George C. Scott attended a fund-raiser for the Seattle Symphony Orchestra. The Vancouver Symphony Orchestra's real-life director at the time, Kazuyoshi Akiyama, conducted the VSO in the movie footage.

The Orpheum also stood in as the location for the Roxbridge International Grand Masters Chess Tournament, where Christopher Lambert challenged Arthur Brauss while trying to predict the moves of a killer in *Knight Moves.*

Plaza of Nations

Features: *Andre, Arctic Blue, Carpool, Pure Luck, Red Scorpion 2, Rumble in the Bronx, Tales of the Crypt: Bordello of Blood*
TV Series: *The Commish, Doctor Who, The Hat Squad, Highlander, Mantis, Neon Rider, The Outer Limits, Sliders, Strange Luck, The X-Files*

The Plaza of Nations (750 Pacific Boulevard South) was built for Expo 86 as a performance area and main entrance. Today the metal-and-glass structure is used for special events and public gatherings. In addition to housing a marina, nightclubs, and offices, the Plaza is also home to Virtue Rekert Studios, a state-of-the-art indoor studio and sound stage that has been employed extensively by many productions.

The Royal Diamond Casino (604-685-2340), one of the Plaza's busiest nightspots, has been featured in many TV series including its recurring role on *Highlander* as a turn-of-the-century San Francisco gambling den.

At The Rage nightclub (604-685-5585), Jackie Chan met up with Françoise Yip, who was dancing in a cage with a real tiger in *Rumble in the Bronx.*

The B.C. Enterprises Building, originally built as the province's pavilion for Expo 86, has also been seen on-screen a few times. It was the Miami airport where Gillian Anderson eluded government agents in an episode of *The X-Files*, the headquarters of Metadyne Pharmaceuticals where Charles Martin Smith worked on viral research in *The Outer Limits*, and the San Francisco Institute of Technological Advancement and Research where time lord Paul McGann borrowed an atomic clock in the TV movie *Doctor Who*.

In the feature comedy *Pure Luck*, Danny Glover starred with Martin Short, a sufferer of "coincidental misfortune syndrome" who fell into a construction hole while walking towards Pacific Boulevard from the Plaza of Nations.

Robson Square

Features: *Bird on a Wire, Bliss, The Changeling, Crying Freeman, Red Scorpion 2, Runaway, Shoot to Kill*
TV Series: *The Commish, Highlander, MacGyver, Madison, Mantis, Strange Luck, The X-Files*

Robson Square, downtown between Hornby and Howe Streets and Georgia and Nelson Streets, was designed by local architect Arthur Erickson and has become one of the city's busiest gathering places. On either end of the complex are the Vancouver Art Gallery and the provincial law courts, with a sunken plaza in between.

Robson Square is one of the city's most popular meeting places, both on and off the silver screen.

Science World's distinctive, and futuristic-looking, geodesic dome.

FBI agent Sidney Poitier and tracker Tom Berenger pursued a kidnapper from Robson Square through the streets of downtown Vancouver. The hostage was Kirstie Alley, and the film was the action thriller *Shoot to Kill*.

Kirstie Alley also spent time at Robson Square in the science-fiction movie *Runaway*. It was here that she fell prey to rock star Gene Simmons while the location doubled as a futuristic outdoor sushi restaurant.

Science World

TV Series: *Earth Star Voyager, Highlander, Mantis, The Outer Limits, Sliders, 21 Jumpstreet, The X-Files*

This high-tech interactive museum (604-268-6363) is easy to find; just look for the large silver golf ball at the east end of False Creek. Its many hands-on displays and scientific demonstrations are fun and informative, and with the world's largest domed theatre screen housed inside its geodesic casing it's also a great place to spend a rainy day. The building's unique shape is very "location specific," but that hasn't stopped the occasional film crew from capturing its twenty-fifth-century look on-screen.

In Disney's science-fiction TV miniseries *Earth Star Voyager*, Science World played a futuristic earth base, while in the science-

Before being released theatrically, some movies go through several name changes. Local examples include *Pals Forever,* which was changed to *Man of the House, Cyberjack,* which became *Virtual Assassins,* and *Glenorky,* which was switched to the innocuous *Magic in the Water.*

fiction TV series *Mantis,* Carl Lumbly time-travelled to the future where the geodesic dome doubled as the headquarters of an evil villain.

In the dimension-hopping TV series *Sliders,* John Rhys-Davies passed swift judgement on the structure by uttering the memorable words, "Now there is a fine example of architectural hubris. A geodesic dome built in an earthquake zone . . ."

And in a fantasy episode of the TV series *21 Jumpstreet,* Science World sparkled in the background while Johnny Depp and Peter DeLuise reminisced about their past.

Sinclair Centre

Features: *Bird on a Wire*
TV Series: *The Commish, Highlander, MacGyver, The Marshal, Robin's Hoods*

Housed in four renovated heritage buildings, this stylish shopping mall and office complex was opened in 1986 after the city's old post office and its extension, the customs building and the historic Winch Office Building were joined together.

In the action comedy *Bird on a Wire,* Mel Gibson and Goldie Hawn took time out from being chased to shop for some ultra-chic designer clothes at a New York City mall. Their boutique of choice—the ultra-chic Leone's.

SkyTrain

Features: *Cousins, Friday the 13th Part 8: Jason Takes Manhattan*
TV Series: *The Hat Squad, Nightmare Cafe, Street Justice, Trial of the Incredible Hulk, 21 Jumpstreet, The X-Files*

Part elevated monorail, part underground subway, Vancouver's rapid-transit system has been running from the Waterfront Station downtown to the city's southeastern suburbs since 1985. Surprisingly, the system isn't used by film companies as often as one might think. Their reason: it's too *clean* to double as a real subway!

In the made-for-TV movie *The Trial of the Incredible Hulk,* Bill Bixby boarded the SkyTrain underground at the Burrard Station. After hulking-out, Lou Ferrigno proceeded to smash up the place.

In the romantic comedy *Cousins,* Ted Danson showed up at the 22nd Street SkyTrain Station and swept Isabella Rossellini off her feet while she awaited her daily work commute.

Who needs Vancouver's spectacular mountain and ocean views anyway? When it comes to big-budget Hollywood features, "Vancouver has some of the best alleyways anywhere in the world," according to *Unforgettable* production designer Rob Pearson.

Vancouver Art Gallery

Features: *The Accused, Bliss, Courting Justice, Crying Freeman, Little Women, Look Who's Talking Now, Power of Attorney, Red Scorpion 2, Russian Roulette*

TV Series: *Birdland, Cobra, The Commish, The Hat Squad, Madison, The Marshal, Neon Rider, The Odyssey, The Outer Limits, Profit, The Round Table, Sliders, Strange Luck, The X-Files*

Originally constructed as a provincial courthouse in 1911, this neoclassical building (750 Hornby Street, 604-682-5621) was spared demolition after a public campaign was launched in the late 1970s. After the new Robson Square law courts were opened in 1979, the building was transformed into an art gallery that now exhibits mostly contemporary art and houses an extensive collection of pieces by celebrated Canadian painter Emily Carr.

The Centennial Fountain was added to the building's front garden in 1966 to commemorate the 1866 union of Vancouver Island with the rest of British Columbia. It was featured in a popular episode of the TV series *Sliders* and could be seen in the show's first season opening credits.

Between the fountain and gallery, three limousines were blown up in the feature *Crying Freeman,* which starred Rae Dawn Chong and Mark Dacascos.

The Vancouver Art Gallery frequently stands in as a courthouse.

Not surprisingly, given its original purpose, the Vancouver Art Gallery doubles mostly as a courthouse, and as such many actors have walked up and down its steps. Among those who have graced the Great Halls of Justice are Jodie Foster and Kelly McGillis in *The Accused,* Leonard Nimoy in *The Outer Limits,* D. B. Sweeney in *Strange Luck,* Michael Chiklis in *The Commish,* and Brian Dennehy in the short-lived TV series *Birdland.*

Yaletown

Features: *Home Movie, Look Who's Talking Too, Rumble in the Bronx, Run, Runaway, Short Time, Urban Safari*
TV Series: *The Commish, Highlander, MacGyver, The Marshal, The Sentinel, Sliders, Strange Luck, 21 Jumpstreet, The X-Files*

Vancouver's warehouse district was originally built during the early 1900s to help service the railway and was named after the Fraser Canyon town of Yale because the CPR moved its locomotive facilities from there to False Creek in the late 1800s. Today, Yaletown is a fashionable urban neighbourhood of upscale retail outlets, trendy eateries, condominiums, and offices. The area has doubled for parts of Manhattan and Seattle, and is bordered by Pacific Boulevard and Homer Street, between Nelson and Drake Streets.

Yaletown is often mistaken for New York City's warehouse district.

In the action comedy *Short Time*, Dabney Coleman recklessly pursued the bad guys through the streets of Seattle in one of the most exciting high-speed car chases ever to be filmed in Vancouver.

Similarly, Pacific Boulevard was the site of extensive chase scenes in two other features. It was the New York street where Jackie Chan piloted a giant hovercraft in *Rumble in the Bronx*, and a futuristic thoroughfare where Tom Selleck and Kirstie Alley were followed by robot trackers in Michael Crichton's science-fiction film *Runaway*.

T•H•E W•E•S•T E•N•D

Features: *Cold Front, Impolite, Intersection, Look Who's Talking, Look Who's Talking Too, Man of the House, Mystery Date, Rumble in the Bronx, Runaway, Russian Roulette, Shoot to Kill, Star 80, Timecop, Underworld, Unforgettable*

TV Series: *The Commish, Danger Bay, The Hat Squad, The Heights, MacGyver, Millennium, The Outer Limits, Profit, Robin's Hoods, Sliders, 21 Jumpstreet, Two, Wiseguy, The X-Files*

Stretching west from Burrard Street, between Coal Harbour and English Bay, is Canada's most densely populated square kilometre. A lively downtown neighbourhood surrounded by parks and beaches is home to Western Canada's largest gay and lesbian population.

Production trucks can often be spotted at Sunset Beach.

Many of the area's older apartment buildings have been featured in films and TV shows, including the often used Kensington Court (1396 Nicola Street) and Hampton Court (1243 Thurlow Street). These two buildings have hosted more than a dozen productions between them, including some episodes of *The Commish* and several TV movies.

Not too far from The Kensington is 1419 Pendrell Street, a recurring site that stands in as Gillian Anderson's Maryland apartment building in the TV series *The X-Files*.

One of the West End's newer buildings, at 1919 Beach Avenue, had a role on the short-lived TV series *Profit*. It doubled as the high-rise home of cutthroat businessman Adrian Pasdar.

Other buildings of note in the West End include the Blue Horizon Hotel on Robson Street, where Eric Roberts was dangled out a window in the docu-drama *Star 80*; the Manhattan Building at Thurlow and Robson, where Kirstie Alley lived in the New York-based comedy *Look Who's Talking*; and Romano's Macaroni Grill (formerly Hy's Mansion) on Davie Street, which posed as the Villa Essex Hotel in the gangster film *Underworld*.

As well, the exterior of Barclay Grocery (1500 Barclay Street) was used for a scene in *Timecop*, and the St. Andrew's Wesley Church (1012 Nelson Street) was where Ray Liotta witnessed the shooting death of Kim Coates after taking a child hostage in the thriller *Unforgettable*.

Across Burrard Street from St. Andrew's Wesley Church is the Wall Centre, another often used location in the TV series *Profit*.

Sunset Beach, at the bottom of Broughton Street off Pacific Boulevard, is a great place to spot film crews. Production "honeywagons" often fill the parking lot while filming occurs on the beach or at nearby buildings. Alexandra Park's Haywood Bandstand, at Harwood and Pacific, is another spot worth keeping an eye on.

In October 1959, matinee film idol Errol Flynn visited Vancouver in hopes of selling his yacht. On his way back to the Vancouver airport he suffered a massive and fatal heart attack and was treated by Dr. Grant Gould, uncle of famous Canadian pianist Glenn Gould.

The Burrard Bridge is sometimes featured as a striking urban backdrop in West End-lensed productions. In the science-fiction film *Runaway*, Tom Selleck drove over the bridge, and Lance Henriksen ran a Seattle-based foot chase on it in the TV series *Millennium*. Some other actors who have performed in the Burrard Bridge's shadow include Richard Gere in the drama *Intersection*, and Jonathan Taylor Thomas and George Wendt in the comedy *Man of the House*.

St. Paul's Hospital and other Vancouver hospitals

Features: *Bliss, Carpool, The Hitman, Look Who's Talking, Unforgettable*
TV Series: *Highlander, Mantis, Profit, The Roundtable, Strange Luck, The X-Files*

One of British Columbia's oldest hospitals, St. Paul's was founded in 1894 by the Sisters of Providence and built on an old dirt road leading to English Bay. Today the Italianate structure stands on the edge of Vancouver's downtown core at 1081 Burrard Street.

In the Seattle-based crime drama *The Hitman*, Chuck Norris was brought back to life in St. Paul's by local actor William B. Davis, better known as *The X-Files'* Cigarette Smoking Man.

In the comedy hit *Look Who's Talking*, New York cabbie John Travolta drove a very pregnant Kirstie Alley to "St. Jerome's Hospital." The doctor who gave her Demerol for her pain was William B. Davis.

> Before appearing in locally filmed productions such as *Rocky IV*, *Street Justice*, and *Happy Gilmore*, action film star Carl Weathers played linebacker for the B.C. Lions' football team.

And in the thriller *Unforgettable*, Ray Liotta had bizarre multi-personality nightmares while Linda Fiorentino stood watch. The doctor on call was again the inimitable William B. Davis!

The area outside the rear of St. Paul's also doubled as the exterior of D. B. Sweeney's loft apartment in the TV series *Strange Luck*.

While St. Paul's is definitely the most recognizable, it is by no means the only Lower Mainland hospital used frequently by the film industry.

The interior of the Vancouver Hospital and Health Sciences Centre (855 West 12th Avenue) has appeared in *The Accused*, *Underworld*, *Unforgettable*, and *The Outer Limits* among others, while the Eagle Ridge Hospital and Health Care Centre (475 Guildford Way) in Port Moody did an extensive stint on the TV series *University Hospital*. The Oakherst Private Hospital (7430 Oak Street) was used by the Canadian independent feature *The Grocer's Wife* as well as *Magic in the Water*, and the Women's Hospital and Health Centre (4500 Oak Street) was featured in the TV movie *Doctor Who*.

Stanley Park

Features: *Another Stakeout, Black Cat 2, Bliss, The Boy Who Could Fly, Crooked Hearts, The Crush, Crying Freeman, Exquisite Tenderness, Fear, Happy Gilmore, Hideaway, The Hitman, Homeward Bound 2, Intersection, Jennifer 8, Jumanji, Little Women, Look Who's Talking, Look Who's Talking Too, Man of the House, Mask of Death, Once in a Blue Moon, Rumble in the Bronx, Timecop, Unforgettable, Who's Harry Crumb?, The Wolfpen Principle*
TV Series: *The Adventures of Beans Baxter, The Commish, The Hat Squad, The Heights, Highlander, The Hitchhiker, Jack's Place, MacGyver, Mantis, The Marshal, Neon Rider, The Odd Couple, The Odyssey, The Outer Limits, Robin's Hoods, The Round Table, Sesame Street, Sliders, Stephen King's It, Strange Luck, Street Justice, 21 Jumpstreet, University Hospital, Unsub, Wiseguy, The X-Files*

Named in honour of Governor General Lord Stanley and opened in 1888, Stanley Park is one of the largest urban parks in the world and is

An independent film production on location at Lost Lagoon.

used every day by thousands of people. Its four hundred hectares of forest land are encircled by a ten-kilometre seawall and ocean beaches. Its diversity and easy accessibility (found to the west of Vancouver's downtown core) make it one of the most frequently filmed spots in the city.

Near the end of the fantasy adventure movie *Jumanji*, Ceperley Meadow was the site where Adam Hann-Byrd threw his Jumanji game off a brick footbridge and into a river. If you look closely, you'll see that the film's river is really just a stream and the bridge is actually made from concrete. The same bridge was used in the family adventure *Homeward Bound 2*, where two of the film's animal heroes went on a "date."

In a rather different date scene, this time at the Brockton Point Lookout, Alicia Silverstone tried to seduce Cary Elwes with a kiss in *The Crush*. Watch for Vancouver's North Shore in the background.

In the science-fiction TV series *Sliders*, the park regularly doubles as San Francisco's Golden Gate Park.

While travelling back in time, Jean-Claude Van Damme and Gloria Reuben wound up in the middle of Lost Lagoon, which stood in as the Potomac River in the science-fiction movie *Timecop*.

One of Danny Glover's first film roles was as a facility assistant in the Vancouver-made sci-fi drama *Iceman*, with leads played by Timothy Hutton and Lindsay Crouse.

Vancouver Aquarium

Features: *Bird on a Wire, Crooked Hearts, Exquisite Tenderness, The Hit Man, Iceman, Short Time, Whale Music*
TV Series: *Cobra, Danger Bay, Jack's Place, Lambchop's Playhouse, MacGyver, Mantis, The Marshal, Strange Luck, The X-Files*

Perhaps best known to television viewers as Donnelly Rhodes's place of work on the syndicated series *Danger Bay*, the Vancouver Aquarium (604-685-3364) at Stanley Park is also renowned for its vast collection of diverse marine life. More than 6,000 species call the aquarium home, including sharks, turtles, seals, sea otters, piranhas, and beluga and killer whales.

In addition to hosting numerous on-site shoots, the aquarium also acts as a studio prop department, renting out such artifacts as whale vertebrae and walrus tusks to productions when needed.

The whale tank is a favoured location. In the drama *Crooked Hearts*, Jennifer Jason Leigh first set eyes on Peter Berg here. For the horror film *Exquisite Tenderness*, the beluga tank area was converted into a restaurant, and in the TV series *Strange Luck* and *The X-Files* it became an office boardroom.

In the science-fiction drama *Iceman*, corridors behind the aquarium's tropical fish tanks were turned into a remote Arctic research facility where Timothy Hutton and Lindsay Crouse thawed out prehistoric caveman John Lone.

W•E•S•T S•I•D•E

B.C. Research Inc.

Features: *Andre, Black Cat, Deep Rising, Far from Home: The Adventures of Yellow Dog, Friday the 13th Part 8: Jason Takes Manhattan, Gold Diggers: The Secret of Bear Mountain, Hideaway, Jumanji*
TV Series: *Nightmare Cafe, The X-Files*

This engineering facility is best known to filmmakers for having the only wave tank in the Pacific Northwest. B.C. Research Inc. (3650

Westbrook Mall) also designed and built the mobile camera dolly used for filming high-speed events at the 1994 Winter Olympics in Lillehammer, Norway. Public access inside the site is restricted, but its location at the edge of the Pacific Spirit Regional Park on the University of British Columbia Endowment Lands makes a great place for a bike ride.

In a scene filmed for the Vancouver-based drama *Intersection*, Richard Gere was supposed to sail under the Lions Gate Bridge on his way from the Lonsdale Quay to the SeaBus terminal. Needless to say, this roundabout trip proved to be so logistically absurd it was left on the cutting-room floor.

Jeff Goldblum's fatal car crash at the beginning of the science-fiction thriller *Hideaway* was staged in the ocean engineering centre's giant wave tank. It was here that he and Christine Lahti were swept into the deadly currents of a raging Washington State river.

In the fantasy adventure film *Jumanji*, Robin Williams's New Hampshire home was engulfed by a monsoon while he and Bonnie Hunt, Kirsten Dunst, and Jonathan Hyde played the board game of the same name. It took several million dollars and more than two months to build and shoot the spectacular three-minute scene.

City Square

Features: *Black Cat 2, Fear, Stakeout, Stay Tuned, Timecop*
TV Series: *The X-Files*

What used to be a pair of turn-of-the-century school buildings (West 12th Avenue and Cambie Street) is now an office and shopping complex, renovated and housed within the old heritage structure opposite Vancouver City Hall. City Square is worth a visit, if not for its innovative architecture and great shops then definitely to check out the gym where Jean-Claude Van Damme worked out between takes on the *Timecop* set. Major sequences from the movie's beginning and end took place here as Van Damme travelled back in time to warn his wife, Mia Sara, about the future.

"Marky" Mark Wahlberg also stalked Reese Witherspoon at this location in the thriller *Fear*.

Before its renovation, City Square's exterior doubled as the Seattle police department headquarters in the comedy *Stakeout*. Here Richard

Dreyfuss and Emilio Estevez got their surveillance assignment from local actor Jackson Davies.

> One of the very first government production facilities to be set up anywhere in North America was in British Columbia. The year was 1920 and its name was the B.C. Patriotic & Educational Picture Service. The BCPEPS collapsed a year later due to an alleged misuse of funds.

Granville Island and False Creek

Features: *Another Stakeout, Cold Front, Cousins, Impolite, Intersection, Reckoning, Rumble in the Bronx, Stakeout, Who's Harry Crumb?*
TV Series: *The Commish, Madison, Neon Rider, The Outer Limits, Profit, Robin's Hoods, The X-Files*

Granville Island isn't so much an island as the result of dredging in False Creek at the turn of the century. This area tucked away at the south end of the Granville Bridge was transformed from its former industrial decrepitude in the late 1970s into the vibrant arts and entertainment centre it is today. Its restaurants, theatres, shops, artists' studios and, of course, the famous Granville Island Public Market all help make it a very popular waterfront spot with locals and visitors.

Similarly, the de-industrialization of False Creek (stretching east from the Burrard Bridge) resulted in international recognition during Expo 86. The False Creek waterfront is now a scenic backdrop to many offices and residences.

In the comedy *Stakeout* and its sequel *Another Stakeout*, Richard Dreyfuss's Seattle waterfront condo (with a view of B.C. Place Stadium!) was actually located at the Moberly Apartments (619 Moberly Road), right around the corner from Monk McQueen's restaurant.

At the east end of False Creek, Jackie Chan water-skied behind a giant hovercraft in the action picture *Rumble in the Bronx*. Watch for the Plaza of Nations, B.C. Place Stadium, and Science World, all visible in the background.

During a shopping trip to Granville Island in the romantic comedy *Cousins*, Isabella Rossellini watched Ted Danson assault a fish in the public market, a sight that's surprisingly not all that uncommon on a busy Saturday afternoon.

Jericho Park, Beach, and Pier

Features: *The Crush, Intersection, The Raffle, Rumble in the Bronx*
TV Series: *Cobra, Highlander, Madison, Trial of the Incredible Hulk, 21 Jumpstreet, University Hospital, The X-Files*

Once the strategic playground of Canada's National Defence Department, Jericho (shortened from "Jerry's Cove") is now a forty-five-hectare public park at the western end of Point Grey Road between English Bay and Fourth Avenue in Kitsilano. Windsurfers, swimmers, sunbathers, bird-watchers, and joggers can escape to this natural setting without leaving the city. Film crews appreciate Jericho for its diversity and convenience.

In the action movie *Rumble in the Bronx,* Jericho Beach was the site of a hilarious scene involving Jackie Chan and an out-of-control hovercraft. It was here that Chan rescued a little girl just before being squashed by the immense vehicle.

The nearby Jericho Sailing Centre (1300 Discovery Street, 604-224-4177) has had many on-screen incarnations. It doubled as a naval hospital and Norwegian bar for *The X-Files,* as well as a bait and tackle shop for the syndicated TV series *Cobra*. The Sailing Centre's personnel have also been called upon to supply skilled windsurfers and sailors for features such as *Mystery Date.*

A Vancouver Film School crew captures the scenery at Jericho Beach.

Kitsilano

Features: *Big Bully, Cold Front, The Crush, Fear, The Grocer's Wife, Immediate Family, Intersection, Magic in the Water, Man of the House, The Raffle, Rumble in the Bronx, Stakeout, That Cold Day in the Park, Trial of the Incredible Hulk*
TV Series: *Cobra, Danger Bay, The Heights, Highlander, JJ Starbuck, Jack's Place, MacGyver, Madison, Millennium, Neon Rider, The Outer Limits, The Roundtable, Sliders, 21 Jumpstreet, University Hospital, The X-Files*

Kitsilano, named for the Squamish chief Khahtsahlano, is one of the most laid-back spots in an admittedly laid-back city. Stretching from the waterfront to 16th Avenue between Alma and Burrard Streets, Kits was home to the Squamish band in the 1800s, the hippie movement in the 1960s and 1970s, and a lot of upmarket cafés, shops, restaurants, and coffee bars for its predominantly well-heeled urban professional population today.

Of all the Kitsilano character houses that have been seen on-screen, the best recognized are from the comedy hit *Stakeout*: 2220 and 2221 Stephens Street, between 6th and 7th Avenues. Here Richard Dreyfuss and Emilio Estevez had Madeleine Stowe's house under sur-

A Kitsilano character house featured in the movie *Stakeout*.

veillance while awaiting the arrival of her escaped-convict boyfriend Aidan Quinn.

The locations featured in Robert Altman's Vancouver-based drama *That Cold Day in the Park* include the Killarney Manor (2890 Point Grey Road) and Tatlow Park (south of Point Grey Road between MacDonald and Bayswater). Sandy Dennis's obsessive relationship with Michael Burns began—and ended—that cold day in Tatlow Park.

Before scoring a hit with the TV series *Quantum Leap*, Scott Bakula starred in a made-in-Vancouver TV pilot called *Indestructible Man*.

Not too far from the park is The Wellington (2630 York Avenue), a recurring site that doubles as David Duchovny's Maryland apartment building in the TV series *The X-Files*.

At 2550 West 10th Avenue stands the Kitsilano Senior Secondary School where Tom Arnold and Rick Moranis battled out their differences in the big-screen comedy *Big Bully*. Though a lot of the Hastings Middle School scenes were filmed at nearby Lord Byng Secondary (3939 West 16th Avenue), Kits High provided many interior hallways for Arnold and Moranis to run around in.

Kitsilano Beach and Park is a lively spot just west of the Burrard Bridge's south end. During the summer it's the "in" place for Vancouver's young and beautiful to be seen. Among the many famous faces who have graced the shores of Kits Beach on-screen are James Woods, Glenn Close, Mary Stuart Masterson, and Kevin Dillon in *Immediate Family*, and Donnelly Rhodes in *Danger Bay*.

The Molson Brewery, at 1515 Burrard Street, has seen its share of star turns as well, including footage in the thriller *Fear* and the family adventure *Magic in the Water*. An actual cave was constructed inside the brewery to house Glenorky, the sea monster!

Pacific Space Centre H. R. MacMillan Planetarium and Vanier Park

TV Series: *Doctor Who, Foxfire, Highlander, MacGyver, Madison, Robin's Hoods, Sesame Street, Sirens, Tales from the Monkey House, 21 Jumpstreet, Wiseguy, The X-Files*

Designed after the conical-shaped hats worn by Northwest Coast Natives, the H. R. MacMillan Planetarium (604-738-7827) at Vanier

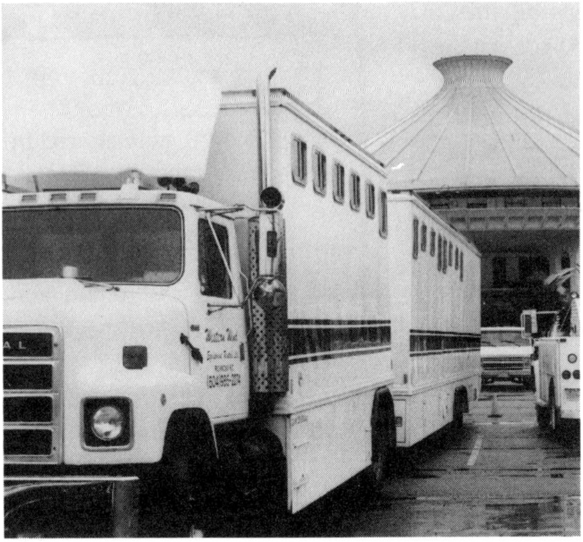

Highlander "honeywagons" parked in front of the Pacific Space Centre.

Park in Kitsilano has become a distinctive English Bay landmark and a reminder that the land upon which it sits was once a First Nations village. Inside the Pacific Space Centre is a state-of-the-art theatre for exploring the cosmos as well as the fascinating Vancouver Museum (604-736-4431).

Because the planetarium is so architecturally distinct and therefore very "location specific," its interior has been used more than its exterior. The outside *did* appear in an episode of *MacGyver*, however. Extras equipped with suitcases walked in and out of the building while it doubled nicely as an international airport terminal.

Science-fiction fans showed up at the Pacific Space Centre while the *Doctor Who* television movie crew was parked in its lot. No one caught a glimpse of the new time lord, Paul McGann, however, because the actual location shoot occurred at a nearby condominium.

Pacific Spirit Regional Park

Features: *Bad Company, Bird on a Wire, The Crush, Crying Freeman, Ernest Rides Again, Harmony Cats, Leaving Normal, North of Pittsburgh, Run, Short Time*
TV Series: *The Black Stallion, The Commish, Mantis, Palace Guard, Robin's Hoods, Sliders, 21 Jumpstreet, The X-Files*

This 763-hectare parcel of forest next to the University of British Columbia is twice the size of Stanley Park but used by far fewer people. Its countless trails and abundance of wildlife, as well as its close proximity to downtown, make it a prime destination for hikers, naturalists, and filmmakers.

Old Marine Drive and Acadia Beach are the busiest spots for production in the park. TV series such as *21 Jumpstreet* and *The X-Files* have been repeat users.

Vancouver's SeaBus terminal (at Cordova and Seymour Streets), originally home to the Canadian Pacific Railway's western terminus, was the sight of Hollywood hysteria when silent-screen newlyweds Vilma Banky and Rod La Rocque passed through in 1927. In the 1940s, Vancouverites swarmed the terminal when Ginger Rogers was vacationing.

Queen Elizabeth Park

Features: *Bliss, The Boy Who Could Fly, Harmony Cats, The Hunted, Rumble in the Bronx, Short Time*
TV Series: *Robin's Hoods, The X-Files*

This stunningly landscaped park at the apex of Vancouver's "Little Mountain" (east of Cambie Street between 29th and 37th Avenues) boasts beautiful sunken rock gardens (a legacy of the park's former incarnation as a quarry) and a spectacular view of the city. It is also home to the Bloedel Floral Conservatory (604-257-8570), a large plexiglass dome that houses myriad tropical plants, flowers, and birds.

In the fantasy drama *The Boy Who Could Fly*, Lucy Deakins reached for a white rose and fell off one of the park's footbridge railings. Fortunately, the "flying" Jay Underwood was there to save her.

After meeting in a Japanese bar, Joan Chen and Christopher Lambert went to watch a taiko drums performance at Queen Elizabeth Park in the thriller *The Hunted*.

Shaughnessy

Features: *Bliss, The Changeling, Crying Freeman, Exception to the Rule, Excess Baggage, Happy Gilmore, Hideaway, Immediate Family, Jumanji, Legends of the Fall, Little Women, Man with a Gun, North of Pittsburgh, One Minute Before Death, Unforgettable, Whale Music, Who's Harry Crumb?*

TV Series: *The Commish, Highlander, MacGyver, Madison, Sliders, 21 Jumpstreet, Wiseguy, The X-Files*

The city's most prestigious residential area stretches east from Arbutus Avenue to Oak Street and north from 41st to 16th Avenues. The film industry loves its palatial mansions and large heritage homes, especially Shaughnessy's most pristine enclave, The Cresent, found at the southeast corner of Granville Street and 16th Avenue. It is here, around the grassy oval park area, that homes like The Hollies and Hycroft Mansion have found their way onto the silver screen.

The darling of the Shaughnessy locales is Hycroft Mansion, located just off The Crescent at 1489 McRae Avenue. This classically designed structure was once home to politician and businessman A. D. McRae. In the 1940s and 1950s, Hycroft served as a veterans' hospital before becoming the University Women's Club in the 1960s.

Today the film industry can't get enough of Hycroft: its interior doubled as a cocktail lounge in Adam Sandler's comedy *Happy Gilmore*, and as several different sets in *Little Women*. It was Maury Chaykin's west coast Howl Mansion in *Whale Music* and a big glitzy Los Angeles home in John Candy's comedy *Who's Harry Crumb*? It has also been seen as an embassy on *The X-Files* and as a college on

Shaughnessy's most often filmed location is the classically designed Hycroft Mansion.

Madison, as well as logging countless appearances in TV movies and television commercials.

Across The Crescent from Hycroft is The Hollies (1388 The Crescent), a grand old turn-of-the-century home that was once occupied by the general manager of the Pacific Great Eastern Railway. Reminiscent of nineteenth-century American classical revival houses, its several TV and movie appearances have included a stint on *Sliders*, as well as standing in for the Plumfield Estate in *Little Women*. Winona Ryder was so taken with the house she wanted to live in it while working in Vancouver. She had to settle for the Sutton Place Hotel.

Want to become part of a "live studio audience?" Keep an eye on the Canadian Broadcasting Corporation (604-662-6000). When the CBC produces specials and current affairs programs requiring in-studio audiences, they use newspapers, radio, and television to spread the word.

A few blocks away, at 1690 Matthews Avenue, is the unusual house known as Glen Brae. Built in 1910 by a Scottish lumber tycoon, Glen Brae was briefly the western Canadian headquarters for the Ku Klux Klan but is now home to Canuck Place, the first free-standing

The feature film *Little Women* utilized The Hollies.

Glen Brae was featured in the motion picture *Legends of the Fall.*

children's hospice in North America. Glen Brae can be seen in its original splendour in the epic drama *Legends of the Fall*. It was here that Brad Pitt visited Julia Ormond at Aidan Quinn's Montana home.

In the fantasy film *Jumanji*, Robin Williams's Brantford, New Hampshire, home was located in the 1400 block of Balfour Avenue, two lots east of Granville Street. Unfortunately, the Parrish House no longer stands, not because of the damage inflicted upon it in the movie but because it was only a false-fronted set built on a vacant lot.

University of British Columbia

Features: *The Accused, Bird on a Wire, Bliss, Carnal Knowledge, Cousins, The Crush, The Fly 2, Intersection, Look Who's Talking, Malicious, Run, Short Time*
TV Series: *Constable Constable, JJ Starbuck, MacGyver, Murphy's Law, Perry Mason, The Sentinel, Sliders, Trial of the Incredible Hulk, 21 Jumpstreet, The X-Files*

The University of British Columbia was founded in 1908 but didn't officially open its doors until 1925, when a massive student protest encouraged the provincial government to follow through with its commitment to higher learning.

Given its location at the tip of Point Grey, UBC offers many remarkable spots for filmmakers to set up camp. The Ladner Clock Tower and Main Library are often called upon for film shoots, as are the chemistry and mathematics buildings and scenic Cecil Green Park. The sprawling campus also boasts a variety of architecturally interesting buildings, including the TRIUMF facility, where the world's largest cyclotron can be found, and the Arthur Erickson-designed Museum of Anthropology (604-822-3825).

> Made-in-Vancouver movies that had their names changed before being released theatrically include *Daddy's Home*, which was switched to *Look Who's Talking*, *Parental Guidance*, which turned into *Immediate Family*, and *Mountain King*, which became *Shoot to Kill*.

The Museum of Anthropology was the backdrop for a confrontational scene involving Alicia Silverstone and Cary Elwes in *The Crush*, as well as an awkward, love-triangle meeting between Richard Gere, Sharon Stone, and Lolita Davidovich in *Intersection*. Watch closely for the museum's establishing shot in *Intersection*: the pond in which the building is reflected is actually a piece of mirror held up to the camera's lens.

Jack Nicholson and Art Garfunkel exchanged theories on their sexual dilemmas while walking along a snow-covered path behind the Student Union Building in the landmark drama *Carnal Knowledge*.

In the drama *The Accused*, UBC doubled as the University of Washington, where Kelly McGillis tried to persuade Bernie Coulson to testify in defense of Jodie Foster.

The university's Theological Centre stood in as Linda Fiorentino's Northern Washington State University research laboratory in the thriller *Unforgettable*. It took the film's special effects team more than three weeks to design and execute a stunt in which the building's interior blows up without anything actually being damaged.

Vancouver City Hall

Features: *Man of the House, Rumble in the Bronx, Underworld*
TV Series: *Strange Luck, Wiseguy, The X-Files*

Vancouver's City Hall building at 435 West 12th Avenue was erected in the mid-1930s, and its location, somewhat off the beaten track at that time, was controversial. But ultimately this site helped connect the newly annexed South Vancouver to the rest of the city. Today the fine Art Deco structure remains the hub of the city's government.

In the action movie *Rumble in the Bronx*, the exterior of the site doubled as a New York police department building, while in the comedy *Man of the House*, City Hall stood in as a Seattle Federal Courthouse where Chevy Chase, playing an attorney, prosecuted mobsters for drug trafficking.

E•A•S•T S•I•D•E

Chinatown

Features: *Bird on a Wire, Bliss, Cousins, Harmony Cats, Homeward Bound 2, Immediate Family, Look Who's Talking, Look Who's Talking Now, Mystery Date, The NeverEnding Story 3, North of Pittsburgh, Red Scorpion 2, Russian Roulette, Unforgettable, Year of the Dragon*
TV Series: *Birdland, The Commish, Danger Bay, Doctor Who, Highlander, MacGyver, Madison, The Marshal, Murphy's Law, Neon Rider, Sliders, Unsub, The X-Files*

Though most of its merchants frown upon location shooting during the hectic business day, historic Chinatown still feels like a film set with its busy streets, bright colours, and lively atmosphere. Van-

Chinatown's colourful streets feel like a movie set, even when crews *aren't* filming.

couver's Chinese community is the city's largest and fastest-growing ethnic group, as well as its oldest. You'll find historic buildings on Pender and Keefer Streets between Carrall and Gore Streets, while most of the exotic food markets are located east of Main.

In a surprising change of pace, the 1953 film *The Desperate Search* starring Howard Keel was set in British Columbia but *wasn't* filmed here. Rather, Oregon played the Canadian province on-screen.

In the Mickey Rourke, John Lone action film *Year of the Dragon*, Vancouver streets were dressed up to stand in for New York's Chinatown. Many key scenes were then matched to Manhattan-lensed footage.

This mix-and-match approach was also used in the family adventure movie *Homeward Bound 2*. A scene in which the film's animal heroes are chased away by a Vancouver store proprietor was later matched with similar footage shot in San Francisco.

The city by the bay was also the setting for the television movie *Doctor Who*, but it was in Vancouver's Chinatown that Sylvester McCoy's time-travelling "tardis" actually landed.

In the romantic comedy *Cousins*, Ted Danson, Sean Young, and Keith Coogan all lived in a Chinatown apartment found in the back of an East Vancouver alley. Several neon signs were installed to make the location look a little brighter and more lively than it was.

One of Chinatown's more popular attractions is the Dr. Sun Yat-Sen Classical Chinese Garden at 578 Carrall Street near Pender (604-689-7133). Fifty-two Chinese artisans spent more than a year creating the Ming Dynasty-style classical garden. It is now a sanctuary for many wishing to escape the hustle and bustle of Chinatown, but watch out for film crews. This unique location is in high demand and has been seen in many movies and in TV shows such as *Highlander* and *MacGyver*.

Exhibition Park

Features: *The Accused, Bird on a Wire, Carpool, Fear, Happy Gilmore, Hideaway, Rocky IV, Run, Star 80, Stay Tuned, Who's Harry Crumb?*
TV Series: *Airwolf, The Black Stallion, Cobra, Highlander, MacGyver, Neon Rider, Strange Luck, Traps, 21 Jumpstreet*

Since 1910, Exhibition Park has carried on the tradition of providing old-fashioned fun amid the city's growing urban landscape. Here you

Some made-in-Vancouver television series have gone through name changes before making it to the tube. *Neon Rider* was originally called *Dude*, *Madison* was known as *High School Lives*, and *21 Jumpstreet* started off as *Jumpstreet Chapel*.

will find the Pacific National Exhibition (although plans are afoot to move the exhibition in 1998), which runs from mid-August to Labour Day, the Playland Family Fun Park, Exhibition Park Racetrack, and the Pacific Coliseum just north of Hastings Street between Renfrew and Cassiar Streets.

The park provides a great variety of indoor and outdoor locations for film companies, and the Agrodome is one of the more popular of these locations. It was used as a wrestling ring by John Ritter and Pam Dawber in the comedy *Stay Tuned*, and as a Moscow boxing arena where Sylvester Stallone fought Dolph Lundgren—and won—in *Rocky IV*. The star of *MacGyver*, Richard Dean Anderson, even used to rent ice time in the building so he and his crew could play hockey.

At the Exhibition Park racetrack, John Candy went undercover as a jockey (yes, a jockey) and got stuck in a phone booth in the comedy *Who's Harry Crumb?*

In the golf comedy *Happy Gilmore*, Carl Weathers taught Adam Sandler how to putt at Playland's miniature golf course, but don't expect to find the "earthquake hole" at "Happy Land." It was just a set.

The park's wooden roller coaster has also been featured in a couple of Seattle-based thrillers. It was the above-ground location for Jeremy Sisto's underground lair in *Hideaway*, and the site of a wild ride taken by "Marky" Mark Wahlberg and Reese Witherspoon in *Fear*.

Mountain View Cemetery

Features: *Bingo, Bullet Proof Heart, Cousins, Crooked Hearts, The Grocer's Wife, Short Time*
TV Series: *Booker, The Commish, The Hat Squad, The Heights, Highlander, MacGyver, Mom P.I., Neon Rider, The Round Table, Scene of the Crime, Stir Crazy, 21 Jumpstreet, Wiseguy, The X-Files*

Vancouver's oldest cemetery was farmland before it started operating in 1887. It now spans forty-two hectares between Fraser and Prince Edward Streets north of 31st Avenue and holds more than ten thou-

Mountain View Cemetery is often the site of spooky film shoots.

sand graves. Some of the city's more famous residents to be interred here include Malcolm Alexander MacLean, the first mayor of Vancouver; Joe Fortes, the legendary English Bay lifeguard; and Robertha Josephine Marshal, who died in 1993 having survived the 1912 Titanic disaster.

For many film crews, the prospect of working in a cemetery can be an unsettling experience. Occasionally, extra tombstones are erected to augment the landscape, which sometimes leads to confusion for visiting relatives. During the TV series *Stir Crazy*, digging an extra hole in the ground became a logistical nightmare when it was discovered the cemetery was already filled to capacity. The hole was dug anyway—carefully.

Despite these occurrences, Mountain View Cemetery is very "film friendly" and has seen its share of Hollywood stars. Before becoming a successful doctor on the TV series *E.R.*, a young Noah Wyle was struck by a car in the Tacoma-based drama *Crooked Hearts*. He was buried in the Mountain View Cemetery by his on-screen family Peter Coyote, Cindy Pickett, Peter Berg, and Juliette Lewis.

During the funeral scene for George Coe in the romantic comedy *Cousins*, Lloyd Bridges showed up and wasted no time pulling out a couple of porno magazines to peruse with his equally bored grandson, played by Keith Coogan.

While performing in Vancouver during the 1950s, the legendary Jack Benny was once mistakenly booked into a hotel suite reserved for a wedding party. Always a master of self-promotion, he called a press conference and graciously gave up the room. He later told Vancouver impresario Hugh Pickett that he didn't want the room anyway because "it was too big"!

Via Rail Train Station

Features: *Cousins, Narrow Margin, North of Pittsburgh*
TV Series: *The Commish, MacGyver, The Marshal, Stephen King's It, The X-Files*

Built by the Canadian Northern Pacific Railway in 1919, this neo-classical-style building at the corner of Station and Main Streets was originally home to Canada's second transcontinental railroad. The terminal has been used repeatedly by made-for-TV movies and television shows, and in the thriller *Narrow Margin.* The Via Rail passenger train bound for Vancouver that Gene Hackman and Anne Archer travelled on while trying to elude James B. Sikking was really a series of cars provided by a Texas collector.

N•O•R•T•H S•H•O•R•E

Capilano River Regional Park

Features: *Big Bully, First Blood, Gold Diggers: The Secret of Bear Mountain, Man of the House, McCabe and Mrs. Miller, Red Scorpion 2, Ski School 2, Watchers*
TV Series: *The Commish, MacGyver, Sliders, Stir Crazy, Highlander, The X-Files*

Stretching from the base of Grouse Mountain down to Marine Drive on the North Shore, Capilano River Regional Park is one of the oldest and most visited parks in the Lower Mainland. Rugged river rapids, the Capilano Suspension Bridge (604-985-7474), the massive Cleveland Dam, and the Capilano Fish Hatchery can all be found within the spectacular canyon park's 160 hectares.

Doubling as an Oregon forest, the woods next to the Cleveland Dam were used for the massive National Guard encampment scenes in the drama *First Blood*. It was in the canyon itself that Sylvester Stallone hid out from the likes of Brian Dennehy and his no-good deputies.

A complete northwest mining town was constructed near Capilano Canyon for director Robert Altman's classic western *McCabe and Mrs. Miller,* which starred Warren Beatty and Julie Christie. A housing development called Cypress Estates now stands where the town used to be.

The park's suspension bridge has also been featured in many productions, including an episode of the TV series *Sliders,* where it became a gateway to a castle in an alternative dimension.

Oops! Take 3: While filming *Rumble in the Bronx,* Jackie Chan was accidentally run over by a hovercraft when he missed jumping into a hole during a stunt. Miraculously he wasn't hurt, but he did injure his ankle later while jumping from a bridge onto the hovercraft.

Deep Cove, Indian Arm, and Burrard Inlet

Features: *Andre, Beyond the Stars, Carpool, Deadly Vows, Gold Diggers: The Secret of Bear Mountain, Mixed Blessings*
TV Series: *The Commish, Danger Bay, The Marshal, Robin's Hoods*

Close to Vancouver, off the Dollarton and Mount Seymour Highways on the North Shore, the peaceful waterfront community of Deep Cove

Deep Cove's tranquil setting is appreciated by locals and filmmakers alike.

Not all Hollywood directors are tyrants. After principal photography on the Vancouver-based feature *Intersection* wrapped, director Mark Rydell rewarded each of his crew with a silver key clasp and a note that read, "Having you on our production was the key to our success."

is nestled between the mountains and waters of Indian Arm. The area offers plenty of options (boating, fishing, hiking, shopping, or dining) at a pace so relaxed many visitors end up staying longer than they had planned.

Tina Majorino and her flippered friend caught the attention of this community as they danced to the "Peppermint Twist" near Deep Cove's government wharf in the family drama *Andre*. The Rockport, Maine, restaurant called Ellwynn's Chowder House, which Tina's on-screen dad Keith Carradine frequented, was actually part of a set built at the Sunset Marina.

Just north of Deep Cove, at the end of Indian River Road, you will find the house featured in the television series *Danger Bay*. If you rent a boat from Deep Cove you can get a better view from the water.

Nearby Cates Park (Roche Point off the Dollarton Highway) has also been featured in many movies and TV series, including *Robin's Hoods* and *The Marshal*. It's a great respite for city dwellers and has all the amenities that most sunbathers and scuba divers require.

Hereditary Squamish Chief Dan George once lived in the area and is buried at the Burrard Indian Reserve cemetery on the north side of the Dollarton Highway. He is perhaps best remembered for his Academy Award-nominated performance opposite Dustin Hoffman in the classic western *Little Big Man*.

Lighthouse Park

Features: *Bad Company, Crying Freeman, Far from Home: The Adventures of Yellow Dog, Fear, Immediate Family, Intersection, Man with a Gun, Mask of Death, Needful Things*
TV Series: *Highlander, The Outer Limits, The X-Files*

Home to the historic Point Atkinson Lighthouse, this wilderness haven in West Vancouver is visited by bird-watchers, hikers, and tourists alike for its rocky cliffs, five-hundred-year-old Douglas firs, and spectacular views of English Bay and the Strait of Georgia. Its easy accessibility doesn't escape the budget-conscious eye of filmmakers either.

In the thriller *Needful Things*, the Point Atkinson Lighthouse took on a foreboding aura whenever Max von Sydow stepped into its shadow to ponder the fate of Castle Rock's townsfolk.

Mary Stuart Masterson and Kevin Dillon spent a reflective moment overlooking English Bay and the lighthouse while they sat on a rocky bluff and talked about the baby they were to give up for adoption in the drama *Immediate Family*.

Directors find the Strait of Georgia makes a breathtaking backdrop when filming at Point Atkinson Lighthouse.

Lions Gate Bridge

Features: *Chaindance, The Hitman, Mystery Date, Russian Roulette*
TV Series: *Danger Bay, Highlander*

Stretching over the Burrard Inlet from the North Shore to Stanley Park, the Lions Gate Bridge was built during the late 1930s and spans some 450 metres. It has become one of the city's most cherished landmarks and remains one of the longest suspension bridges in the world. Its graceful form has often been captured on-screen and it has been crossed by many movie stars.

In the drama *Chaindance*, Michael Ironside drove cerebral palsy sufferer Brad Dourif over the bridge to the big city for an ultimately fatal encounter with a prostitute.

Ethan Hawke and Teri Polo drove across the Lions Gate and into a whole heap of trouble in the comedy *Mystery Date*.

In the suspense drama *Russian Roulette*, in which Vancouver actually plays Vancouver, George Segal fought our infamous rush-hour traffic (even in 1975!) on his way to stop an assassination.

And Chuck Norris contemplated his fate in front of the bridge just before a covert meeting with Ken Pogue in the crime drama *The Hitman*.

Lower Lonsdale

Features: *Bird on a Wire, Cold Front, Far from Home: The Adventures of Yellow Dog, Intersection, Man of the House*
TV Series: *The Adventures of Beans Baxter, The Commish, MacGyver, Mantis, The Marshal, The Odyssey, Sliders, 21 Jumpstreet, The X-Files*

At the turn of the century, North Vancouver's industrial waterfront area was booming and a number of buildings, stretching from Burrard Inlet to 3rd Street along Lonsdale Avenue, were constructed. Thankfully, they still survive, and this historic Lower Lonsdale area is a major destination for shoppers and tourists. A quick trip across Burrard Inlet from the downtown SeaBus terminal can have you at the Lonsdale Quay Public Market within minutes. The area's close proximity to the North Shore Studios makes Lower Lonsdale a great place for a film shoot.

While trying to elude bad guys in the action comedy *Bird on a Wire,* Mel Gibson and Goldie Hawn narrowly made their escape by driving along Esplanade to Lonsdale, which miraculously led to a New York City freeway.

One too many pratfalls didn't stop Chevy Chase from driving his out-of-control truck down Lonsdale, through Versatile Pacific Shipyards, and into Burrard Inlet in the comedy *Man of the House.*

Many car chases have been filmed in the vicinity of Lonsdale Avenue.

Lynn Canyon Park

Features: *The Hunted, Jumanji, Magic in the Water, Watchers*
TV Series: *The Commish, Hawkeye*

Within Lynn Canyon Park's 250 hectares are a genuine suspension bridge, stunning forest trails, and an Ecology Centre (604-981-3103) for the environmentally curious. You'll find the park and Lynn Creek, a popular yet dangerous spot frequented by swimmers and divers, north of Lynn Valley Road, off the Upper Levels Highway in North Vancouver.

In the action film *The Hunted*, Lynn Canyon Park doubled as the site of the Mikado clan's secret Ninja camp, where John Lone won back the respect of his men by fighting and killing Ninja Ken Kensei.

And at nearby Lynn Headwaters, Robin Williams toiled with a stubborn pelican to retrieve his Jumanji game in the fantasy film *Jumanji*.

> More than six thousand people are directly employed by the film production industry in Vancouver. Thousands more benefit from its spinoff effects. And as British Columbia's film production revenue approaches $500 million annually, spinoff spending usually triples that figure, bringing the province's yearly total to nearly $1.5 billion.

The North Shore Mountains
Cypress Bowl, Grouse Mountain and Mount Seymour

Features: *The Changeling, Crackerjack, Narrow Margin, Roxanne, Russian Roulette*
TV Series: *Cobra, The Fall Guy, MacGyver, The Outer Limits, The X-Files*

Whether you want to clamber up their winding trails during the summer, swoosh down them in the winter, or just gaze at them from just about any place in the city, the North Shore mountains are all things to all people: playground, backdrop, landmark. Within minutes you can be atop any one of these magnificent peaks.

Just off the Upper Levels Highway in West Vancouver is the North Shore's westernmost mountain, Cypress Bowl (604-926-5612). At 1,450 metres it has the steepest vertical drop of the three ski hills.

In *The Changeling*, Cypress Bowl's snow-covered access highway doubled as the upstate New York road where George C. Scott's wife

The Ranger's Station at Mount Seymour.

and child (Jean Marsh and Michelle Martin) were tragically killed, prompting him to move to a haunted house in Seattle.

The North Shore's middle mountain, Grouse, can be found at the top of Capilano Road in North Vancouver. Principally a hill for novice and intermediate skiers, Grouse (604-984-0661) is 1,128 metres high and offers a whole lot more than just skiing. Take the Skyride to the top of the peak and you'll find mountaintop dining, helicopter tours, multimedia shows, and hiking trails with spectacular views of the Lower Mainland.

You'll also find the place where Gene Hackman and M. Emmet Walsh came looking for Anne Archer in the action film *Narrow Margin*, and where Gillian Anderson was abducted by "aliens" in a popular episode of *The X-Files*.

As well, George Segal's unmarked police car was towed from the top of the mountain's skylift in the thriller *Russian Roulette*.

Mount Seymour (604-986-2261), the North Shore's easternmost mountain, is thirteen kilometres up the Mount Seymour Road. During the summer, hike up Dinkey Peak for magnificent views of Indian Arm and Washington State. In the winter months skiing lessons are well attended by both young and old. The fourteen-hundred-metre-high mountain is also popular with snowboarders.

The Mount Seymour Ranger's Station has been featured in *The Outer Limits* and *The X-Files* TV series.

Before becoming part of the successful medical TV series *E.R.*, both Noah Wyle and Gloria Reuben starred in movies made in Vancouver. Wyle played Peter Berg's younger brother in the drama *Crooked Hearts*, and Reuben was Jean-Claude Van Damme's time-travelling police partner in *Timecop*.

The North Shore Studios

Features: *Bliss, Far from Home: The Adventures of Yellow Dog, Gold Diggers: The Secret of Bear Mountain, Happy Gilmore, Harmony Cats, Impolite, Intersection, Jennifer 8, Little Women, Look Who's Talking Too, Man of the House, Needful Things, North of Pittsburgh, Pure Luck, Run, Tales from the Crypt: Bordello of Blood, This Boy's Life, Whale Music*

TV Series: *The Black Stallion, Cobra, The Commish, The Hat Squad, Jack's Place, The Marshal, Nightmare Cafe, Profit, Strange Luck, Street Justice, Traps, 21 Jumpstreet, Two, Wiseguy, The X-Files*

Relatively young by Hollywood standards, the North Shore Studios was started up by television producer Stephen J. Cannell in the late

The North Shore Studios' impressive arched gateway.

Buster Keaton's final film appearance was in the 1965 National Film Board production *The Railrodder*, a twenty-five minute short that featured Keaton on an east-west journey across Canada. B.C. footage included the Rockies and North Vancouver.

eighties and opened its doors to the film community in 1989. Its seven sound stages and wrap-around façades have been utilized by television series, features, and made-for-TV movies, as well as music videos and commercials. The largest production centre of its kind in Canada, the North Shore Studios is located behind a small shopping centre at 555 Brooksbank Avenue in North Vancouver. Though public access is restricted, you get a great behind-the-scenes view of the lot from above on Heywood Street near Keith Road.

The studios' many sound stages and street façades double as Anywhere, USA, or anywhere in the world, for that matter.

Concrete, Washington, the boyhood home of real-life writer Tobias Wolff, who was portrayed in the drama *This Boy's Life* by Leonardo DiCaprio, was re-created in part on the North Shore Studios lot. Robert De Niro and Ellen Barkin co-starred.

A gargoyle's loft, a frozen Alaskan wasteland, and a secret UFO storage facility have also been re-created at the North Shore Studios—all for the TV series *The X-Files*.

Seymour Demonstration Forest

Features: *Big Bully, The Hunted, Jumanji, Little Women, Man of the House, Tales from the Crypt: Bordello of Blood*
TV Series: *The Commish, Hawkeye, Highlander, Madison, Mantis, The Marshal, Millennium, The Outer Limits, Poltergeist: The Legacy, Strange Luck, Two, The X-Files*

Opened to the public in 1987, this 5,600-hectare area is part of Vancouver's watershed system.

Every year there can be upwards of a hundred days of filming in the forest, and its convenient location (north of the Mount Seymour Parkway off Lillooet Road in North Vancouver) makes it readily accessible for productions based at the North Shore Studios.

In the Massachusetts-based drama *Little Women*, Kirsten Dunst almost drowned when she fell through a frozen pond in the forest.

Luckily Winona Ryder and Christian Bale were there to save her. Later in the film, Ryder turned down Bale's marriage proposal in a scene also shot here.

The forest handily doubled as a woods in Japan in the action movie *The Hunted*. Here in the Ninja camp of the Kinjo clan Christopher Lambert lay low and learned the art of swordfighting. The forest was also the site of the film's climactic sword battle between John Lone, Christopher Lambert, and Yoshio Harada.

Versatile Pacific Shipyards

Features: *Alaska, Another Stakeout, Bounty Hunters, Bullet Proof Heart, Dream Man, The Hitman, Homeward Bound 2, Man of the House, Man with a Gun, Mask of Death, North of Pittsburgh, Timecop, Unforgettable*
TV Series: *Cobra, The Commish, Highlander, Mantis, The Marshal, Millennium, The Odyssey, Once a Thief, The Outer Limits, Sliders, The X-Files*

This former dry dock to the east of Lonsdale Quay in North Vancouver was founded at the turn of the century and became home to the largest ship manufacturer in Canada. More than half the ships in the Canadian Navy's fleet were built here during the Second World War, as well as several ferries and arctic icebreakers. Though ship construction

A small mountain was constructed inside Versatile Pacific Shipyards' old machine shop for the movie *Alaska*.

stopped in the early nineties, the shipyard is still used frequently by film companies looking for a unique industrial waterfront setting.

Maritime history buffs may wish to visit North Vancouver's Museum and Archive (209 West 4th Street, 604-987-5618) for more information; the heritage site itself is currently inaccessible to the public.

> The very first experimental film to be shot in Vancouver was made in 1943 by two women, Dorothy Fowler and Margaret Roberts. Their short film had an equally short title: *and.*

For the adventure film *Alaska*, set builders actually constructed a small snow-capped mountain inside the shipyard's old machine shop. It was the largest interior space available at the time and perfect for the film's crashed plane sequence.

In the science-fiction film *Timecop*, one of the shipyard's warehouses played the Parker McComb Datalink Building, where Ron Silver time-travelled to the past and paid himself a visit, while in the adventure movie *Homeward Bound 2*, the shipyard doubled as the San Francisco waterfront where the film's animal heroes took refuge. If you look closely during these scenes, Vancouver's skyline is clearly visible in the background.

As well, in the thriller *Unforgettable*, Ray Liotta flashed back to an execution-style murder that Peter Coyote and Garwin Sanford undertook in one of the shipyard's warehouses.

—S•E•A T•O S•K•Y C•O•R•R•I•D•O•R—

Features: *Alive, Distant Thunder, Free Willy 3, Happy Gilmore, Intersection, Leaving Normal, Narrow Margin, Shoot to Kill, Stay Tuned, White Fang 2*
TV Series: *The Outer Limits, The Sentinel, The X-Files*

Stretching from Horseshoe Bay to Whistler, the hundred-kilometre-long Sea to Sky Corridor (featured prominently in the opening scenes of *Intersection*) winds its way past breathtaking mountain vistas and sleepy bedroom communities toward the internationally renowned ski resort.

Nineteen kilometres north of Lions Bay is the Furry Creek Golf and Country Club, where Adam Sandler and Bob Barker were part-

The Sea to Sky Corridor reveals scenic Howe Sound.

nered together for a celebrity golf tournament in the comedy *Happy Gilmore* and eventually ended up in a hilarious big-screen brawl.

In the thriller *Narrow Margin*, the Sea to Sky Corridor was the site of a dramatic train ride that featured Gene Hackman, Anne Archer, and James B. Sikking. The same train line was also used in the TV series *The X-Files*, where a boxcar was blown up at Porteau Cove.

Britannia Beach

Features: *Arctic Blue, Distant Thunder, Excess Baggage, Friday the 13th Part 8: Jason Takes Manhattan, Gold Diggers: The Secret of Bear Mountain, Hideaway, Intersection, Leaving Normal, Look Who's Talking Now, Red Scorpion 2, This Boy's Life, We're No Angels, White Fang 2*
TV Series: *Airwolf, Cobra, Highlander, MacGyver, The Outer Limits, Poltergeist: The Legacy, 21 Jumpstreet, The Twilight Zone, Wiseguy, The X-Files*

On the coast of Howe Sound, forty-five minutes north of Vancouver's Studio Zone, sits the somnolent community of Britannia Beach. Formerly a mining town and the British Empire's largest processor of copper during the 1930s, it's now home to the B.C. Museum of Mining, a national historic site where live equipment demonstrations

A short drive from Vancouver is the B.C. Museum of Mining, an often used film location.

and underground tours are given. (Open seasonally, 604-688-8735.)

The B.C. Museum of Mining may not be filled with gold, but when its underground tunnels were featured in the coming-of-age adventure *Gold Diggers: The Secret of Bear Mountain*, Christina Ricci and Anna Chlumsky had little difficulty tapping its veins and coming out filthy rich by film's end! Similarly, it played an Alaskan gold mine where Scott Bairstow faced off with Alfred Molina in *White Fang 2*.

The interior of the mining museum also served as a place of refuge for Leonardo DiCaprio and his pals in the drama *This Boy's Life*, and it doubled as the Blackridge Penitentiary from which Robert De Niro and Sean Penn escaped during the opening scenes of the comedy *We're No Angels*.

Anchored across the highway from the museum is an old cruise ship called the *Prince George*. Among its many claims to fame is its appearance in the eighth *Friday the 13th* installment, *Jason Takes Manhattan*. It doubled as a cruise ship full of teens who were stalked by the man in the goalie mask.

Britannia Beach's Ninety Niner Restaurant (playing itself) was where Richard Gere stopped to write a "Dear Jane" letter to Lolita Davidovich in the drama *Intersection*. It also stood in for Dave's Truck Stop, where Christine Lahti, Meg Tilly, Maury Chaykin, and Lenny Von Dohlen chowed down in the road movie *Leaving Normal*.

Horseshoe Bay, Bowen Island and the Sunshine Coast

Features: *Another Stakeout, Deadly Sins, Devotion, Homeward Bound 2, Immediate Family, Needful Things, The Russia House, The Stepfather, Watchers*
TV Series: *The Beachcombers, Madison, The Marshal, The Outer Limits*

In 1987, producer Patrick Hasburgh *(21 Jumpstreet)* told *Reel West Magazine* that Vancouver would become "the film capital of the world in 10 years." Since then, the city has in fact become the largest production centre for episodic television outside Hollywood.

Twenty minutes north of Vancouver, off the Sea to Sky Highway, is the BC Ferry Terminal at Horseshoe Bay. Here you can catch ferries across Howe Sound to filming locales like Bowen Island and the Sunshine Coast. The terminal itself has played a Seattle ferry dock in *Another Stakeout.*

In *The Russia House,* Roy Scheider, J. T. Walsh, and John Mahoney all put the screws to Soviet sympathizer Sean Connery in an interrogation scene that took place at a waterfront home on a secluded Pacific Northwest island. The house is really on the north coast of Bowen

Molly's Reach restaurant was a recurring location in the CBC television series *The Beachcombers.*

> Some British Columbians who've made it big in Hollywood include Yvonne De Carlo, Raymond Burr, Michael J. Fox, Dorothy Stratten, Meg and Jennifer Tilly, Jason Priestly, Bruce Greenwood, Cameron Bancroft, Kim Cattrall, Pamela Anderson Lee, James Doohan, and Helen Shaver.

Island, close to Hood Point, and if you look closely during this scene you'll see a ferry sailing in the background.

Bowen Island also doubled as Washington State's Bainbridge Island, where Richard Dreyfuss, Emilio Estevez, and Rosie O'Donnell were on *Another Stakeout.* The houses used are located at Fairweather Point.

In *Needful Things,* Gibsons on the Sunshine Coast stood in for Castle Rock, Maine, where antique store proprietor Max von Sydow pitted the town's inhabitants against each other. The fictional town's church, which went up in flames during the movie's spectacular climax, was built at the Travel Infocentre near School Road and Marine Drive.

Gibsons is no stranger to the rigours of filming. For nineteen years it played a major role in the internationally syndicated CBC television series *The Beachcombers.* You'll find "Molly's Reach" (604-886-9710), the restaurant where Bruno Gerussi and Robert Clothier spent their time, at the intersections of School Road, Gower Point Road, and Marine Drive.

Squamish

Features: *Distant Thunder, Jennifer 8, Leaving Normal*
TV Series: *The X-Files*

The town of Squamish (about an hour north of Vancouver's Studio Zone on Highway 99) was originally a logging community. Today the area is a prime destination for rock climbers who come from around the world to scale the infamous Stawamus Chief, the second largest free-standing granite outcropping in the world (the Rock of Gibraltar is the biggest).

In the drama *Distant Thunder,* Vietnam War veteran John Lithgow battled demons from his past as he worked at an Olympic Peninsula wood mill (located in Squamish) while awaiting a visit from his estranged son, played by Ralph Macchio.

Squamish's wood mill was featured in the movie *Distant Thunder*.

Whytecliff Park

Features: *Andre, Another Stakeout, Crying Freeman, Fear, Mask of Death, Whale Music*

Whytecliff Park at the western tip of the North Shore is designated the only underwater reserve in the province. Its protected bay is home to an amazing array of marine life and is a prime destination for scuba divers from all over the world. Sheltered beaches and landscaped play areas are also very popular with visitors and filmmakers.

In the drama *Whale Music,* many coastal exteriors for Maury Chaykin's waterfront mansion were shot here, but don't expect to find the house itself; it was actually Hycroft Mansion in Shaughnessy.

B•U•R•N•A•B•Y

The Bridge Studios

Features: *The Air Up There, Alive, Another Stakeout, Bad Company, Big Bully, Bird on a Wire, The Boy Who Could Fly, Clan of the Cave Bear, Cousins, The Crush, The Experts, First Blood, The Fly 2, Iceman, Jumanji, Leaving Normal, Legends of the Fall, Look Who's Talking Now, Motherlode, Narrow Margin, Roxanne, Runaway, Shoot to Kill, Spacehunter: Adventures in the Forbidden Zone, Stay Tuned, Timecop*

TV Series: *The Adventures of Beans Baxter, The Death of the Incredible Hulk, Doctor Who, Highlander, JJ Starbuck, MacGyver, The Outer Limits, Poltergeist: The Legacy, The Trial of the Incredible Hulk*

Originally built in the 1930s as a construction facility for the Lions Gate and Golden Gate Bridges, the massive building that now holds the Bridge Studios' special effects stage was later taken over by BC Hydro as a storage depot. The early eighties saw the location used in films such as *First Blood, Spacehunter,* and *Iceman* before the studio officially opened in 1987. Today, the busy studio (2400 Boundary Road, just north of the Lougheed Highway in Burnaby) spans six hectares and holds four sound stages as well as the largest effects stage in North America.

> In 1899, D. W. Griffith's legendary cameraman Billy Bitzer came to British Columbia and captured footage of the spectacular Rocky Mountains. His boss at the time, American inventor and motion picture producer Thomas Edison, was so impressed that he returned the following year to film the Rockies himself.

The unassuming entry gate to the Bridge Studios.

The elaborate time-travel launch pad for *Timecop* was built on the John Thomas Special Effects Stage. So were the immense zoo and jungle sets for *Bird on a Wire* and *Jumanji*, the interior airplane fuselage for *Alive*, and Philip Sterling's high-tech lab for what would be one of Bill Bixby's last major projects, *The Death of the Incredible Hulk*.

Oops! Take 4: While filming a routine explosion effect for the TV series *The Sentinel*, several windows in downtown Vancouver office buildings were accidentally shattered. The cause was determined to be a combination of unseasonably cold weather and a larger-than-planned explosion.

Central Park

Features: *Happy Gilmore, Mystery Date*
TV Series: *Highlander, MacGyver, Midnight Heat, Robin's Hoods, The X-Files*

Central Park, a landmark since 1891, is one of the Lower Mainland's most treasured parks. You'll find it just west of Metrotown, between Kingsway and Imperial Avenue in Burnaby. It has bike trails and picnic areas, playgrounds, a small lake, and many sporting facilities, including Swanguard Stadium (604-435-7121), the home of the Vancouver 86ers' soccer team.

Recently renovated, Swanguard Stadium has hosted several productions, including a unique venture by Electronic Arts Canada. It was here that Vancouver 86ers' soccer star Carl Valentine was filmed, then digitally scanned so he could be incorporated into a video game based on the World Cup.

Deer Lake Park

Features: *Cousins, Intersection, Kissed, Timecop*
TV Series: *Highlander, The Hitchhiker, MacGyver, Stephen King's It, 21 Jumpstreet, The X-Files*

This popular urban refuge, where visitors pilot pedal boats and kayaks along the lake's wooded shoreline, is located in central Burnaby off Canada Way. The Hart House Restaurant (604-298-4278) and the Burnaby Art Gallery (604-291-9441), both of which have been used by

The Loftus House at Deer Lake was nicknamed "the Cousins' house" by Vancouver film crews.

film companies, are on hand for those who prefer to do their relaxing indoors.

The park is also home to Burnaby's Heritage Village and Carousel, a two-hectare turn-of-the-century B.C. hamlet re-created to simulate small-town life circa 1900. Though it looks like a freshly painted movie set, it's actually a museum with operating shops, historic locomotives, and authentically costumed guides. (Open seasonally from April to September, 604-293-6501.)

In the TV miniseries *Stephen King's It*, Jonathan Brandis and his friends glimpsed the frightening antics of Pennywise the Clown as Tim Curry pranced through the Heritage Village streets in full circus attire.

The romantic comedy *Cousins* filmed several of the park's locations, including the lake itself, where Ted Danson and Isabella Rossellini took time out from their courtship to have a swim. The Loftus House on Deer Lake Avenue, which has since been nicknamed "the Cousins' house" by local film folk who shoot there, was featured in a wedding reception scene.

Farther along Deer Lake Avenue is where Jean-Claude Van Damme's beautiful Washington, D.C., house blew up in the science-fiction movie *Timecop*. Largo Entertainment spent more than a quarter million dollars constructing the Victorian-style mansion in the parking lot of the Burnaby Art Centre's James Cowan Theatre (6450 Deer Lake Avenue). The Walker residence actually had to be built *twice*—

after blowing it up the first time, the filmmakers decided the explosion had been too big!

Simon Fraser University

Features: *American Boyfriends, Bad Company, Double Happiness, The Fly 2, Intersection, Watchers*
TV Series: *Death of the Incredible Hulk, The Ground Star Conspiracy, The Marshal, The Odyssey, The Outer Limits, Sliders, The X-Files*

While shooting the John Candy comedy *Who's Harry Crumb?*, the film's crew always had four palm trees with them so at any given time the Lower Mainland could stand in for sunny L.A.

Located on the south side of Burnaby Mountain, Simon Fraser University was designed by world-renowned Vancouver architect Arthur Erickson and opened in 1965. A unique structure even by today's standards, its modern look has not gone unnoticed and has been used to a great extent in many science-fiction and futuristic movies and TV shows.

The science-fiction thriller *The Fly 2* employed SFU's campus as the Bartok Industries Research Facility, where Daphne Zuniga fell in love with Eric Stoltz *before* he turned into a giant fly.

In the made-for-TV movie *Death of the Incredible Hulk*, SFU doubled as the exterior of Genecore Laboratories, where Bill Bixby and Philip Sterling experimented with gamma radiation.

Before heading south to attend her cousin's wedding, Margaret Langrick and her friends briefly attended a class on the SFU campus (actually playing the SFU campus) in the coming-of-age drama *American Boyfriends*. But what's with all the scaffolding and workmen in this scene? Well, the locally based sequel to *My American Cousin* took place in the 1960s while the school was still under construction.

R•I•C•H•M•O•N•D

Features: *Cousins, Crash, Deadly Sins, The Hunted, Jennifer 8, Knight Moves, Rumble in the Bronx, Stay Tuned, Stephen King's It, Who's Harry Crumb?*
TV Series: *The Adventures of Beans Baxter, The Commish, Danger Bay, General Hospital, Highlander, Huckleberry Finn and His Friends, MacGyver, The Marshal, The Odyssey, The Sentinel, Sliders, Two, The X-Files*

A crew from the made-in-Vancouver television movie *A Child's Wish* flew to the White House where U.S. president Bill Clinton made a cameo appearance in their production.

This former agricultural community is now home to the largest Chinese population in Canada. Its many attractions include the serene Buddhist Temple, historic Steveston Village, and the charming Minoru Chapel where George Coe and Norma Aleandro got hitched at the beginning of the romantic comedy *Cousins*.

Richmond's old-fashioned show garden Fantasy Garden World (604-277-7777), next to the Steveston Highway Interchange off Highway 99, looks like a Hollywood movie set and has had the time on-screen to prove it.

In the romantic comedy *Cousins*, Fantasy Garden World doubled as "Wedding Land," where Isabella Rossellini's husband, William Petersen, flew into a drunken rage while Sean Young and Ted Danson looked on during a family wedding reception.

The action film *Rumble in the Bronx* also filmed a wedding scene here, during which Anita Mui enlisted the help of Jackie Chan to help run his honeymoon-bound uncle's supermarket.

In an episode of the TV series *Sliders*, the Garden's village façade was the site of one of the show's many parallel-earth settings.

Fantasy Garden World looks like a freshly painted movie set.

A film crew on location in front of Steveston's popular Net Shed café.

Steveston Village

Features: *Crash, The Hunted, Jennifer 8, Knight Moves, Stay Tuned, Who's Harry Crumb?*
TV Series: *Danger Bay, General Hospital, Highlander, Huckleberry Finn and His Friends, MacGyver, The Marshal, The Odyssey, Sliders, Two, The X-Files*

For location spotters, this historic fishing village in the southwest corner of Richmond is a must-see not only for its varied turn-of-the-century architecture, but also for its quaint shops and fresh off-the-docks fish sales. Founded in 1889 by William Steves, the community still thrives as a functioning port, cannery, and major tourist attraction.

Many of Steveston's heritage sites have been used repeatedly by the film industry. The Gulf of Georgia Cannery (12138 4th Avenue) stood in as a warehouse on the TV soap *General Hospital*, the Britannia Heritage Shipyard (1241 Trites Road) has been seen in many shows including *MacGyver* and *The X-Files*, and Garry Point Park was the site of a western-style hanging in the *Highlander* TV series.

The big-budget thriller *Jennifer 8* employed several locations, including London Farm, which doubled as the home of Lance Henriksen and Kathy Baker. The Marine Garage on historic Moncton Street played a key role in Andy Garcia's police investigation; after hearing a pedestrian crossing signal, Garcia came to one of the film's many plot-turning revelations. Visitors to Moncton Street may have their own revelation; there are no audible traffic signals in Steveston, only stop signs.

> Before making it big with *The Kids in the Hall* and *NewsRadio* TV series, Dave Foley made his movie debut as a cub reporter in the 1986 Vancouver-made film noir spoof *High Stakes*.

Vancouver International Airport

Features: *The Changeling, Crying Freeman, Homeward Bound 2, Little Panda, Look Who's Talking, Look Who's Talking Too, Look Who's Talking Now, Pure Luck, Rumble in the Bronx, Russian Roulette, Who's Harry Crumb?*
TV Series: *MacGyver, The Sentinel, The X-Files*

The Vancouver International Airport opened on Sea Island in Richmond in 1929 and is Canada's second busiest airport. In the mid-1960s, a major expansion was undertaken to accommodate the city's growing international reputation, and today, after a second major expansion to add a luxurious new international terminal, the Vancouver International Airport stands not only as Canada's gateway to the Pacific but to the world. It can also be a great place to spot visiting celebrities.

In the comedies *Pure Luck* and *Who's Harry Crumb?*, SCTV alumni Martin Short and John Candy both had their share of excitement at YVR. Short has a comic confrontation after his luggage is taken, and Candy gets stuck at a security check because of the metal plate in his head.

Vancouver International Airport also stood in as Kennedy International Airport in *Rumble in the Bronx*. And in the family adventure *Homeward Bound 2*, both the main and south terminals doubled as the San Francisco International Airport, where the film's animal heroes found themselves running around on the baggage conveyors and runways.

D•E•L•T•A

Features: *The Accused, Bird on a Wire, Cold Front, Distant Thunder, Ernest Rides Again, The Experts, Jumanji, Shoot to Kill*
TV Series: *The Commish, Death of the Incredible Hulk, Highlander, MacGyver, Madison, The Marshal, Rescue 911, Wiseguy, The X-Files*

The Sidetrack Pub was featured in the motion picture *The Accused.*

The farmland and rural roads of this agricultural suburb, founded by the Ladner brothers in 1868, are popular with filmmakers. So are some other often used film locations such as the historic Ladner Harbour Village, the Reifel Bird Sanctuary, Boundary Bay Airport, and the Tsawwassen Ferry Terminal.

In *The Accused,* Jodie Foster visited the Mill Bar in Birchfield County, Washington, where she was subsequently assaulted. Actually, the scene of the crime was the Sidetrack Pub under the Alex Fraser Bridge at 10190 River Road (604-583-3920).

In the fantasy adventure film *Jumanji,* Robin Williams drove David Alan Grier's police car through the Sir Save-A-Lot Discount Store where all hell was typically breaking loose. The previously vacant building looked so real Tsawwassen residents were disappointed when they learned the new discount store was just a movie set. Ironically, the location was later taken over by Liquidation World (1193 56th Street and 12th Avenue).

The Tsawwassen Ferry Terminal is where you can catch a ferry to the Gulf Islands (where part of the classic *Five Easy Pieces* was shot) or to Victoria, via Swartz Bay, on Vancouver Island. The Tsawwassen terminal has been featured in several TV shows and movies, including *Bird on a Wire* and *Shoot to Kill.*

Tsawwassen's Liquidation World doubled as the Sir Save-A-Lot Discount Store in the big-budget feature *Jumanji.*

S•U•R•R•E•Y

Features: *Cousins, For a Few Lousy Dollars, Happy Gilmore, Homeward Bound 2, Knight Moves, Rumble in the Bronx, Tales from the Crypt: Bordello of Blood*
TV Series: *The Commish, Highlander, MacGyver, Mantis, The Marshal, Rescue 911, Wiseguy, The X-Files*

Surrey is one of Canada's fastest-growing municipalities and sought after by the film industry for its diverse locales. Tynehead Regional Park and the community of Cloverdale are two of the area's more frequently used locations. Some of Surrey's other communities have appeared on-screen so often that one district, Whalley, has dubbed itself "Whalleywood."

In North Surrey, off King Road at 116A Street, the Port Mann Power Plant has doubled as an eerie backdrop in many television movies and other productions, including the series *Mantis* and the horror film *Tales from the Crypt: Bordello of Blood.*

The waterfront communities of White Rock and Crescent Beach have had plenty of screen time too.

The usually peaceful Semiahmoo Park and First Nation Reserve played host to a sideshow full of circus freaks while doubling as a Florida cemetery and trailer park in the popular *X-Files* TV series.

The seaside town of White Rock is a favourite location of many filmmakers.

In the thriller *Knight Moves*, Tom Skerritt's float plane docked at the White Rock Pier when he returned with Daniel Baldwin to investigate a murder, while Crescent Beach stood in for the film's seaside town of Roxbridge, Washington.

— N•E•W W•E•S•T•M•I•N•S•T•E•R —

Features: *Little Women, Matinee, Quarantine, Rumble in the Bronx, Run, Short Time*
TV Series: *Cobra, The Commish, Highlander, MacGyver, The Marshal, The Outer Limits, Stephen King's It, 21 Jumpstreet, Wiseguy, The X-Files*

Named by Queen Victoria in the 1860s, B.C.'s former provincial capital is located between Burnaby and the Fraser River. The "Royal City" is rich in local history and many of its heritage homes have been used in film productions, including the feature *Little Women* and the television miniseries *Stephen King's It*.

Stephen King's It also includes footage shot at Columbia Street and the old Paramount Theatre, where Jonathan Brandis and his pals were chased by the town bullies after they imprudently spilled drinks on them at the local movie house.

Since the 1960s, Vancouver has been a major centre for animation. Hanna-Barbera's series *Abbott and Costello* and *The Beatles* were produced here, as was the more recent International Rocketship production of *The Far Side* TV special. Continuing computer-animated series *Reboot* and *Transformers* are also produced in Vancouver. Walt Disney Animation even has a studio in town, where projects, including a *Beauty and the Beast* sequel, are being made.

The exterior of the Paramount was also featured in the Canadian B movie *Matinee,* where most of its local cast (including *The X-Files'* William B. Davis) was murdered one by one. Interestingly though, interiors were shot at the Vogue theatre downtown.

One of the most exciting car chase sequences to be filmed in the Lower Mainland took place along New Westminster's Front Street, an industrial waterfront thoroughfare that boasts many specialty antique shops. It was here (and in Yaletown) that Dabney Coleman chased the bad guys in the action comedy *Short Time.* Front Street's 500 block was also the site of a motorcycle drag race scene in the action flick *Rumble in the Bronx.*

New Westminster's Front Street has doubled as Seattle and the Bronx.

Formerly a "lunatic asylum," Woodlands School is now used frequently by the film industry.

Woodlands School

Features: *Quarantine*
TV Series: *Cobra, The Commish, Highlander, MacGyver, The Marshal, The Outer Limits, The X-Files*

Built in the 1870s as a psychiatric hospital (known at that time as the Provincial Lunatic Asylum), Woodlands evolved into a rehabilitation centre for mentally challenged children where the innovative "play to learn" program was established. Today, because of mainstreaming and cutbacks, Woodlands (9 East Columbia Street, New Westminster) is operating with a minimal staff and is scheduled to be shut down at the end of 1996.

Like Riverview Hospital in Coquitlam (see next section), Woodlands is used by production companies looking for large interior and exterior spaces that can double as hospitals, prisons, and law offices. The site has been featured in many commercials and music videos, as well as in movies and on television. *The X-Files* used it as a federal penitentiary *and* as a psychiatric hospital.

Features: *Bad Moon, Big Meat Eater, The Boy Who Could Fly, Chaindance, Crying Freeman, Deadly Vows, Exquisite Tenderness, Happy Gilmore, Homeward Bound 2, The Hunted, Jennifer 8, Power of Attorney, Quarantine, Run, Smart Alec, Unforgettable*
TV Series: *Birdland, Cobra, The Commish, Highlander, MacGyver, Mantis, The Outer Limits, Poltergeist: The Legacy, The Sentinel, Stephen King's It, University Hospital, Wiseguy, The X-Files*

The former sawmill towns of Coquitlam, Port Coquitlam, and Port Moody are far enough removed from Vancouver's downtown core to be peaceful, but close enough for thousands of residents to commute to and from work every day. Film companies find them equally convenient when trying to induce a rural Middle-American ambience.

The television series *The Sentinel,* which takes place in the city of Cascade, Washington, stirred things up a bit in Coquitlam's commercial district when North Road was used as the site of a large explosion.

The area's less commercial landmarks have also seen filmmaking action. Lafarge Lake was featured on the TV show *MacGyver,* and Mundy Park got spooked during an episode of *Poltergeist: The Legacy.*

Riverview Hospital's Crease Clinic is one of the busiest studios in the Lower Mainland.

Riverview Hospital

Features: *Bounty Hunters, The Boy Who Could Fly, Chaindance, Deadly Vows, Exquisite Tenderness, Happy Gilmore, The Hunted, Jennifer 8, Matinee, Power of Attorney, Quarantine, Run, Tales from the Crypt: Bordello of Blood, Unforgettable*
TV Series: *Birdland, Cobra, Highlander, Mantis, The Outer Limits, Strange Luck, The X-Files*

In 1984, when *Jurassic Park* writer Michael Crichton was asked why he chose Vancouver as the setting for the futuristic feature *Runaway*, he told *The Hollywood Reporter* ,"It's my idea of the ideal big city of the near future."

Riverview Hospital at 500 Lougheed Highway in Coquitlam was built as a psychiatric hospital for recovering First and Second World War veterans, but has actually become one of the busiest studios in the Lower Mainland. Its Crease Clinic and West Lawn building, shut down in the late 1980s due to streamlining and budget cuts, are used almost daily now by production companies who gladly pay an honorarium to the B.C. Mental Health Society for the chance to use the old character structures.

The private hospital does have a reputation among local film crews for being "haunted," however. The West Lawn site tends to get cold and clammy, and props frequently go bump in the night. An ominous iron-bar casing, which prevented patients from throwing themselves down the building's interior stairwell, serves as a reminder of less fortunate days.

Nonetheless, Riverview has been used repeatedly by TV shows such as *Highlander, The Outer Limits,* and *The X-Files,* as well as for commercials and music videos. It has been dressed up to look like chic apartments, county court rooms, city morgues, and law offices.

It was a school for the blind in the thriller *Jennifer 8*, a Harvard campus in the action film *Run,* and a retirement home in the comedy *Happy Gilmore.*

Mostly, though, it doubles as a prison and hospital, roles for which it is eminently suited. In the drama *Chaindance*, the West Lawn building stood in as the Lennox County Hospital, where cerebral palsy sufferer Brad Dourif met up with inmate Michael Ironside during a prisoner work program. And in the fantasy *The Boy Who Could Fly*, Jay Underwood was committed to Riverview when officials discovered that his grasp on reality was fleeting.

L•A•N•G•L•E•Y

TV Series: *The Black Stallion, Hawkeye, Highlander, The Marshal, Poltergeist: The Legacy, The X-Files*

Forty-seven kilometers east of Vancouver is British Columbia's birthplace: the Fort Langley National Historic Site. It was at Fort Langley, in 1858, that B.C. was officially proclaimed a colony. Today the area's many winding rural roads are very popular with filmmakers as are the Campbell Valley Regional Park, and the historic town of Fort Langley.

The nearby Milner Downs Equestrian Centre (21795 64th Avenue) in Langley was used by *The Black Stallion* TV series for several seasons. Here Mickey Rooney would impart wisdom to anyone who would listen.

T•H•E F•R•A•S•E•R V•A•L•L•E•Y

Features: *The Accused, Big Bully, Empire of Ash 3, First Blood, Gold Diggers: The Secret of Bear Mountain, Happy Gilmore, Homeward Bound 2, Intersection, Jumanji, Needful Things, Timecop, We're No Angels, White Fang 2*
TV Series: *Bordertown, Danger Bay, Highlander, Max Glick, Neon Rider, Poltergeist: The Legacy, Sliders, 21 Jumpstreet, Wiseguy, The X-Files*

The town of Hope, B.C., stood in as Hope, Oregon, in the Rambo movie *First Blood.*

East of Vancouver's Studio Zone, stretching along the Lougheed and Trans-Canada Highways, lie the serene pastures of the Fraser Valley.

Among the many towns that dot the landscape are Abbotsford, where the Abbotsford International Air Show is held every August. The family adventure *Homeward Bound 2* made good use of the town's airport for a scene involving the movie's dog and cat stars and a departing airplane.

Who says Hollywood actors don't have time for their fans? While filming the feature *The Accused* at the Vancouver Hospital and Health Sciences Centre, Jodie Foster took a break from her busy schedule to surprise a terminally ill patient with a special visit.

Maple Ridge's country roads doubled nicely as the Brantford, New Hampshire, setting where David Alan Grier's police car was driven by monkeys and savaged by pachyderms before it was finally pulled into the brush by a giant vine in the fantasy film *Jumanji*.

For the big-budget comedy *We're No Angels*, Paramount Pictures spent $2.6 million creating the 1930s depression-era American town of Brandon. Built on the banks of Stave Lake near the Ruskin Dam, between Maple Ridge and Mission, Brandon was the fictional border town where escaped convicts Robert De Niro and Sean Penn posed as priests while trying to escape to Canada. Demi Moore co-starred as De Niro's love interest. Local residents wanted to keep the faux town as a tourist attraction, but it was torn down after the film wrapped.

Bordertown, on the other hand, has remained intact since the TV series of the same name ended its four-year run in the early nineties. This fully functional western burg at the north end of 224th Street in Maple Ridge is still used by companies wanting to re-create an authentic turn-of-the-century look on-screen.

The Virtue Studio Ranch, where the syndicated TV series *Neon Rider* was filmed, is east of Mission, just up from Cascade Park off Sylvester Road. The private facility covering sixty hectares is a complete, working studio with the latest in high-tech equipment, and boasts mountain ranges, flatlands, lakes, and waterfalls.

In the comedy *Big Bully*, the Cascade Falls doubled as the Vermillion Falls where Rick Moranis confronted Tom Arnold in a breathtaking scene from the film's climax. You'll find the falls at the end of Ridgeview Road, just off Sylvester Road past Mission.

Farther east, you can locate the site of Richard Gere's tragic car crash in the drama *Intersection*, which happened on a rural road in the Deroche area, just past Mission.

At the junction of the Fraser Canyon and Coquihalla Highways is the town of Hope, B.C., which doubled as the town of Hope, Oregon, in the original *Rambo* movie, *First Blood*. Here Vietnam vet Sylvester Stallone turned into a one-man killing machine after being hassled by the local sheriff, played by Brian Dennehy.

David Duchovny and Gillian Anderson as FBI Agents Mulder and Scully in the Vancouver-filmed *X-Files*.

X MARKS THE SPOT

In the spring of 1993 *The X-Files* was in search of a forest. Unable to find one near Los Angeles in which to film the show's pilot episode, the production company decided a trip to Vancouver, British Columbia was the next logical step. The rest, as they say, is history. X-creator Chris Carter fell in love with the city, proclaiming it, "Hollywood's biggest back lot!" Vancouver and the rest of the world fell in love with *The X-Files*.

Never has a television show captured the collective imaginations of its viewing audience quite like this one. Part science fiction, part high drama, and part sardonic comedy, the show X-philes loyally tune into every week, chronicles the lives of FBI agents Fox Mulder (David Duchovny) and Dana Scully (Gillian Anderson) as they chase monsters, aliens, and government conspirators in their continuing search for the truth.

Produced by 20th Century Fox Television and Carter's Ten-Thirteen Productions for the Fox Network, *The X-Files'* phenomenal success has spawned many imitators, but none is as stylishly well made and consistent as the original. The show's success has also rubbed off on Duchovny and Anderson, big-time. They've become international sex symbols and a hot topic for X-phile's chat-group discussions on the Internet.

Fame has also been bestowed upon Vancouver; after all, it's our fair city that stands in for the remote and exotic locales Mulder and Scully travel to week in and week out.

Those real locations have been extensively researched and compiled in this section so that X-philes can travel from Washington, D.C., to Tildeska, Norway, and even Newark, New Jersey, without ever leaving the Lower Mainland. The corresponding episodes in which these places appear are listed in order of their broadcast dates, each with a

Although many productions have called Vancouver home, no genre has done so more than science fiction and fantasy. Notable features have included *The Thing*, *The Fly 2*, *The NeverEnding Story*, *Timecop*, *Hideaway*, and *Jumanji*. TV series include *Highlander*, *Mantis*, *Poltergeist*, *The Odyssey*, *The Outer Limits*, *The Sentinel*, *Sliders*, *The X-Files*, and the *Doctor Who* and *Incredible Hulk* TV movies.

brief description of the events that transpire. The location listings do not include stock footage filmed outside Vancouver, privately owned residential homes, or scenes captured within the confines of the North Shore Studios.

The truth is out there.

The X-Files
Season 1

Pilot

In their first case, FBI agents Fox Mulder and Dana Scully investigate possible alien abductions in an Oregon town.

- ***Simon Fraser University:*** The exterior of FBI Headquarters, Washington, D.C.
- ***BC Hydro Building, 333 Dunsmuir Street:*** The interior lobby of FBI Headquarters. Scully passes through on her way to be assigned "The X-Files."
- ***CBC Building, 700 Hamilton Street:*** The CBC Newsroom stands in for the FBI Bullpen. The CBC Green Room becomes Mulder's office.
- ***SW Marine Drive at the University of British Columbia:*** Bellefleur, Oregon. Mulder and Scully take this route when entering the small coastal town.
- ***Crescent Beach, White Rock:*** Bellefleur, Oregon. Mulder and Scully drive through the town on their way to the cemetery.
- ***Queen Elizabeth Park:*** Bellefleur Cemetery. While exhuming a corpse, Mulder and Scully discover an alien body inside a casket.
- ***Seymour Demonstration Forest:*** Collum National Forest, northwest Oregon. Mulder and Scully investigate the death of Karen Swenson when she is killed after being enveloped by a strange bright light.
- ***Riverview Hospital:*** State Psychiatric Hospital, Ramon County. Mulder believes that the hospital's psychiatric patients are alien abductees.
- ***Cedar Lane Motel, 926 160th Street, White Rock:*** A fire at Mulder and Scully's motel destroys the alien X rays vital to their investigation.

Deep Throat

Did the Air Force kidnap a delusional test pilot? Mulder and Scully's search for answers is stonewalled by mysterious black-suited men when they get too close to the truth.

The *X-Files'* Gillian Anderson and David Duchovny on location in Steveston Village.

- ***The Meatmarket Restaurant, 1 West Cordova Street, Gastown:*** A bar in Washington, D.C., where Mulder first meets with Deep Throat.
- ***Hill Top Cafe, Langley:*** The Flying Saucer Diner, Idaho. Mulder obtains a map showing how to get to the Ellen's Air Base.
- ***Boundary Bay Airport:*** Ellen's Air Base, Idaho. Mulder and Scully witness UFOs performing high-speed manoeuvres. Later, when Mulder witnesses the spacecraft up close, he is abducted and his memory erased.
- ***Erik's Restaurant, 1317 56th Street, Tsawwassen:*** Erik's Restaurant, Idaho. Mulder and Scully get the lowdown on Ellen's Air Base from two teenaged UFO watchers.
- ***South Delta Senior Secondary, 750 53rd Street, Tsawwassen:*** Mulder's second meeting with Deep Throat takes place on a school jogging track.

Squeeze

A friend of Scully's from the FBI Academy puts the detectives onto their first case not involving aliens. This time, their quarry is an Earth-born mutant whose crimes seem to stretch back to 1903.

- *Plaza of Nations, B.C. Club*: Scully has lunch with a sceptical FBI agent.
- *Front Street parking ramp, 560 Columbia Street, New Westminster*: A Baltimore parking garage. Scully and Mulder first encounter Eugene Victor Tooms climbing out of an air duct.

Exiter Street, Baltimore (a Hastings Street alley).

- ***West Hastings Street alley, 55-block:*** 66 Exiter Street, Baltimore. The site of the old condemned building where Eugene Victor Tooms lives.
- ***Riverview Hospital:*** David Hill Sanitarium, Baltimore. Where Eugene Victor Tooms is committed.

Conduit

Mulder's troubled memories of his long-abducted sister come to the forefront when the agents investigate the possible alien abduction of an Iowa teenager.

- ***Simon Fraser University:*** The exterior of FBI Headquarters, Washington, D.C.
- ***Vancouver Art Gallery:*** Sioux City Library. Mulder and Scully follow a girl into a library where she gives them clues about a missing teen.
- ***Pennsylvania Pub, 412 Carrall Street, Gastown:*** Pennsylvania Pub, Sioux City. Mulder and Scully look for Ruby's boyfriend and encounter a bartender sporting a UFO tattoo and a melted ear.
- ***Stay 'N Save Motor Inn, 10551 St. Edwards Drive, Richmond:*** Stay 'N Save Motel, Sioux City. Mulder and Scully encounter National Security agents at their motel.

- *SW Marine Drive, entrance to UBC:* Sioux City freeway. While Mulder explains to Scully why he thinks young Kevin Morris is an alien conduit, they drive past the Sioux City downtown on-ramp.
- *Buntzen Lake, Port Coquitlam:* Lake Okobogee, Iowa. Mulder and Scully investigate a hotbed of UFO sightings and discover the body of Greg Randall. Later they return to find Ruby Morris.
- *Christ Church Cathedral, 690 Burrard Street:* Interior of church where Mulder prays after wrapping up the investigation.

While most Vancouver productions have a main unit involving the principal actors and a smaller second unit used for insert and establishing shots, *The X-Files* actually has a third unit just for "pick-up" shots, virtually unheard of in television.

Jersey Devil

Freudian subtexts get an intriguing workout when Mulder hunts for a vicious feral woman who appears to be dining on Atlantic City derelicts. Meanwhile, the ambivalent Scully pursues a personal relationship.

- *Seymour Demonstration Forest, Twin Bridges:* The woods outside Atlantic City, New Jersey, where the "Jersey Devil" is spotted and later killed by police.
- *Pacific Boulevard:* "Welcome to Atlantic City" sign. Mulder and Scully drive into town to learn more about a recent killing.
- *Station Street:* An Atlantic City street. Mulder trades places with a homeless person to try to glimpse the "Jersey Devil."
- *Adega Cafe, 1022 Main Street:* Atlantic City coffee shop. Mulder tells Scully about what he saw in the alley.
- *Molson Brewery, Kitsilano:* An abandoned Atlantic City warehouse where Mulder, Scully, and the police track down the "Jersey Devil."

Shadows

Imploding throats and guardian angels figure prominently as Mulder and Scully ferret out the truth behind the murders of Iranian terrorists by a seemingly mild-mannered Defense Department secretary.

Who says stereotypes can't be broken? Before William B. Davis landed the role of the sinister Cigarette Smoking Man on *The X-Files,* he played a doctor in the features *The Hitman, Look Who's Talking,* and *Unforgettable.*

- ***Dunsmuir Street at Seymour Street:*** Broad Street, Philadelphia, Pennsylvania. Mulder and Scully investigate the mysterious deaths of two men who attacked Lauren Kyte at a bank machine.
- ***Mountain View Cemetery:*** A Philadelphia cemetery. Mulder and Scully observe Lauren Kyte visit the grave of her dead employer.

Ghost in the Machine

An ominous supercomputer named "Central Operating System" (C.O.S.) achieves the ability to think and the ability to kill! Watch out Mulder! Look over your shoulder, Scully!

- ***Metrotower II, Eaton Centre, Burnaby:*** Eurisko World Headquarters, Washington, D.C. Mulder and Scully investigate a crime scene. Later, Deep Throat meets Mulder outside, where he explains about the Defense Department's artificial intelligence program.
- ***Burnaby Civic Square, Kingsborough Street and Willingdon Avenue, Burnaby:*** Eurisko World Headquarters. Outside Eurisko, Mulder speaks with Scully about the possibility that the C.O.S. computer killed Drake.
- ***Park bench near bus loop at Chilco and Robson Streets:*** Deep Throat and Mulder meet to discuss the future of the Defense Department's artificial intelligence program.

Ice

Mulder, Scully, and three scientists explore an ice core drilling project in which the contractors appear to have killed one another after suffering a severe form of cabin fever.

- ***Delta Park, 120th Street, Surrey:*** Doolittle Airfield, Nome, Alaska. Mulder and Scully charter a plane to take themselves and three scientists to the ice core drilling facility.

Space

A ghostly alien invades the body of a NASA project director, encouraging him to sabotage an upcoming space shuttle launch.

> Fans of *The X-Files* know him as the Cigarette Smoking Man, but William B. Davis also operates the Vancouver-based William Davis Centre For Actors' Study, an acting school for beginners and professionals.

- *Canadian Airlines Hangar, YVR:* Houston Mission Control Building. Mulder and Scully get a quick tour before visiting Mission Control.
- *Robson Square:* Washington, D.C. On the steps of a public square, Mulder and Scully meet covertly with a NASA official who suspects that space shuttle missions are being sabotaged.
- *Mountain View Cemetery:* The site of NASA project director Colonel Belt's military funeral.

Fallen Angel

Mulder meets a man previously abducted by aliens when Deep Throat sends him to Wisconsin to search for a UFO that has crashed.

- *Seymour Demonstration Forest:* Townsend, Wisconsin. The military implements "Operation Falcon" after a UFO crashes in the woods.
- *Lions Gate Travelodge, 2060 Marine Drive, North Vancouver:* The Budget Rest Motel, Townsend, Wisconsin. Mulder and Scully learn more about UFO enthusiast Max Fenig.
- *Simon Fraser University, Academic Quadrangle:* While tracking the invisible alien, several soldiers are burned.
- *Versatile Pacific Shipyards:* Lake Michigan Waterfront, Dock 7. Max Fenig disappears.
- *Simon Fraser University:* FBI Headquarters, Washington, D.C. After Mulder's insubordination hearing, Deep Throat meets with Chairman McGrath outside FBI Headquarters and tells him to "always keep your friends close, but keep your enemies closer."

Eve

Mulder's usual alien abduction hypothesis turns out to be optimistic when the violently disturbed subjects of a forty-year-old genetics experiment come of age and try to fine-tune their bloodlines.

In a Los Angeles-based episode of *The X-Files*, the show's location scouts picked a SW Marine Drive mansion to double for a posh Hollywood pad. The house really belonged to Vancouver Canucks' superstar Pavel Bure.

- ***Lynnwood Marina, 1681 Columbia Street, North Vancouver:*** Mulder meets Deep Throat and learns of the "Litchfield Experiments" involving genetically controlled children.
- ***Riverview Hospital:*** At a sanitarium, one of the "Eve" clones gives Mulder and Scully some background about Dr. Sally Kendrick's genetically engineered children.
- ***Seacrest Motel and RV Park, 864 160th Street, White Rock:*** Seacrest Motel, Pt. Reyes National Seashore, California. Eve 8 brings the twins here after kidnapping them.
- ***Marilee's Cafe, 15782 Marine Drive, White Rock:*** The Hi-Way 49 Cafe. Mulder and Scully are almost poisoned by the twins when they stop for soft drinks.

Fire

A past love interest of Mulder's (now an inspector with Scotland Yard) invites him to join her on the trail of a psychotic pyrotechnic.

- ***Citypark Parkade, Seymour Street:*** Washington, D.C., parking garage, level 6. Mulder and Scully meet up with Phoebe Green, an old Oxford flame of Mulder's.
- ***Loftus House, Deer Lake Park, Burnaby:*** The Cape Cod, Massachusetts, residence of British transplant Sir Malcolm.
- ***Simon Fraser University:*** FBI Headquarters in Washington, D.C.
- ***Seymour Street at Robson:*** Mulder and Green discuss pyrokinetics while walking in the rain.
- ***Hotel Vancouver:*** Interior of the Venable Plaza Hotel, Boston. A fire breaks out while Mulder and Green are slow-dancing.

Beyond the Sea

This time Mulder is the sceptic and Scully the believer as the latter tries to mourn the passing of her father while she and her cohort question a psychic death-row inmate about his link with a serial killer.

- *Garry Point, Steveston:* A seaside funeral service is held for Scully's father.
- *Niagara Hotel, 435 West Pender Street:* Raleigh, North Carolina. Death-row convict Luther Lee Boggs's vision of a waterfall translates into a hotel's neon sign which helps lead Scully to recover a missing teen's necklace.
- *SeaBus terminal:* Raleigh, North Carolina. The "angel of stone" from death-row convict Luther Lee Boggs's vision turns out to be a statue (found in front of the SeaBus terminal).
- *Britannia Heritage Shipyard, Steveston:* Raleigh, North Carolina. Mulder is shot while trying to locate the missing teens.

All in a day's work. When *X-Files* stunt co-ordinator Tony Morelli was set ablaze during the show's third season episode "Pusher," co-star Gillian Anderson was asked to put out the flames with a fire extinguisher. Anderson seemed unfazed by the request and pulled it off without a hitch.

Gender Bender

The tunnels below an Amish-like cult community in Massachusetts may just hold the secret to why so many dance-club kids are ending up dead—killed by animal-secreted pheromones.

- *Twilight Zone, 7 Alexander Street, Gastown:* Germantown, Maryland, dance club, where the murderer picks up his/her unassuming victims.
- *Steveston Village, Richmond:* Steveston, Massachusetts. Mulder and Scully's investigation leads them to where the mysterious Kindred cult resides.
- *Marine Grocery, Moncton Street, Steveston:* Inside a local grocery store, shopkeepers give Mulder and Scully the lowdown on the Kindred.
- *Redden Net Co., Moncton Street, Steveston:* Allen Feed & Tackle Shop. Scully nearly succumbs to the bizarre charm of a young Kindred member named Andrew.
- *Rowlatt Historic Farm, Campbell Valley Regional Park, Langley:* The Kindred Farm. Mulder and Scully discover that strange goings-on are going on beneath the Kindred farm.

Long before Vancouver was known as Hollywood North, the stars came to this area to relax and unwind. John Wayne frequented the Gulf Islands on fishing trips, Bob Hope routinely played golf around the Lower Mainland, and Phyllis Diller came just to get away from L.A.

Lazarus

Scully's former boyfriend, an FBI special agent, asks for her help in solving the case of a pair of bank robbers, one of whom's soul seems to have invaded his.

- ***Bank of Montreal, Granville and Pender Streets:*** The Maryland Marine Bank. FBI agent Jack Willis gets shot in a hold-up while Scully shoots and kills the robber.
- ***Riverview Hospital:*** A research hospital where Mulder and Scully speak with Dr. Barnes about the negative aspects of near-death experiences.
- ***Simon Fraser University:*** Exterior of FBI Headquarters, Washington, D.C.

Young at Heart

A man from Mulder's past, the killer of a fellow FBI agent who Mulder failed to stop years earlier, shows up in Washington, D.C.

- ***Granville Street at Georgia Street:*** Exterior of Washington, D.C., crime scene. Mulder and Scully are called to investigate a murder.
- ***Bollum's Books:*** Washington, D.C., crime scene. While investigating the robbery and murder, Mulder finds a piece of evidence that spooks him.
- ***Vancouver Centre Mall:*** Outside the Washington, D.C., crime scene. Mulder gives Scully the background on John Barnett.
- ***Mahon Park, North Vancouver:*** Mulder receives some photos and a death threat when he returns to his car.
- ***Riverview Hospital:*** Tashmoo Federal Correctional Facility. Mulder and Scully discover that John Barnett is not dead.
- ***Rose & Thorne Pub, 755 Richards Street:*** Gertie's Pub. Deep Throat meets with Mulder to tell him about the government's involvement with John Barnett.
- ***Orpheum Theatre:*** Interior of the Janie Taylor Memorial Recital Hall, Washington, D.C. While acting as bait to capture John Barnett, Scully gets shot.

- *Via Rail Station:* Washington, D.C., train station. John Barnett stashes the secret fountain of youth progeria information in locker 935.

X-*Files* creator Chris Carter, who christened Vancouver "Hollywood's biggest back lot," is so pleased with the city he chose to film his latest TV series, *Millennium,* here as well.

E.B.E.

Deep Throat plays a disturbing game of trust with Mulder when he confides to the agent that a truck carrying an "extra-terrestrial biological entity" (or E.B.E.) is crossing the United States toward an unknown destination.

- *Seymour Demonstration Forest:* Lexington, Tennessee. Mulder and Scully investigate multiple UFO sightings.
- *The Wellington, 2630 York Avenue:* Alexandria, Maryland. Mulder's apartment building. Mulder puts a light in his window to contact Deep Throat.
- *Science World Promenade:* Lincoln Memorial, Washington, D.C. Deep Throat meets Mulder and gives him a top-secret document.
- *Simon Fraser University:* Exterior of FBI Headquarters, Washington, D.C.
- *Vancouver Aquarium:* Deep Throat and Mulder meet in front of a shark tank to discuss a forged photograph.
- *1100-block Homer Street:* Scully catches a cab and Mulder drives erratically to try to lose men following him.
- *SW Marine Drive, UBC:* Junction 90 and 283, Washington State. Mulder and Scully catch up with the truck.
- *Powertech Labs Inc., Surrey:* Mattawa, Washington. Mulder and Scully gain access to a secret government installation where Mulder learns more about Deep Throat.

Miracle Man

If a charismatic Tennessee faith healer isn't killing members of his flock with the laying on of his hands, who is?

- *100-block, 1st Street West, North Vancouver:* Kenwood, Tennessee, 1983. During a raging fire, young Samuel Hartley brings a burn victim back to life.

Several of the actors who appeared on David Lynch's weird TV series *Twin Peaks* have also appeared on Chris Carter's weird TV series *The X-Files*. Included are Kenneth Welsh, Michael Anderson, Michael Horse, Don Davis, Jan D'Arcy, and, of course, David Duchovny.

- ***Steveston Village, Richmond:*** Kenwood, Tennessee. Mulder and Scully are called in to investigate the murder of a woman at the hands of Samuel Hartley.
- ***Marine Garage and 2nd Avenue, Steveston:*** Kenwood, Tennessee. Site of the Miracle Ministry's tent.
- ***Rusty Gull Pub, 175 East 1st, North Vancouver:*** At a Kenwood bar, Mulder and Scully meet Samuel who tells Mulder about his sister.
- ***Riverview Hospital:*** Kenwood County Courthouse and Jail. A swarm of locusts invade the courthouse during Samuel's hearing.

Shapes

Mulder and Scully investigate paranormal murders on an Indian reservation. Could it be the work of . . . a manitou?

- ***Bordertown, Mission:*** Trego Indian Reservation, northwest Montana. Mulder and Scully meet with Sheriff Tskany and examine the body of a shooting victim.
- ***Seymour Demonstration Forest, mid-valley point:*** Funeral pyre. Mulder tells Scully of the J. Edgar Hoover X-File that is similar to their own.

Darkness Falls

Mulder and Scully momentarily forget their survival skills when they investigate the disappearance of loggers and find a big ugly batch of green prehistoric bugs who like to dine on *Homo sapiens.*

- ***Lighthouse Park:*** Olympic National Forest in Washington State where Mulder and Scully try to locate the missing loggers.

Tooms

Mulder and Scully do double time dealing with both the omnipresent Cigarette Smoking Man *and* the liver-eating cretin from "Squeeze," who has returned for seconds after being released from the local psychiatric ward.

- ***Heather Street near Vancouver Health Sciences Centre:*** Baltimore, Massachusetts. Mulder spooks Tooms on the street.
- ***City Square Mall, 555 West 12th Avenue:*** 66 Exiter Street, Baltimore. Eugene Victor Tooms returns home to hibernate for another thirty years, but his apartment building has been turned into a shopping mall. He is killed by Mulder and Scully in the escalator.

Born Again

Mulder is convinced a telekinetic child must be the reincarnation of a dead cop.

- ***Abbott Street, 200 block, Gastown:*** 14th Precinct House, Buffalo, New York. Mulder and Scully investigate the "jumping" death of a police officer.
- ***Riverview Hospital:*** Brylin Psychiatric Hospital. Mulder learns more about the little girl, Michelle.

Exiter Street, Baltimore (City Square Mall).

- *1st Street West, North Vancouver:* Downtown Buffalo. While Michelle rides a bus, a man becomes caught in the door and is killed.

Roland

A mentally challenged janitor attracts the agents' attention when he answers the murderous telepathic commands of the cryogenically preserved head of his evil twin.

- *B.C. Research Inc.:* Mahan Propulsion Laboratory, Washington Institute of Technology, Colson, Washington. Mulder and Scully investigate the death of an aeronautical engineer at the facility where Roland works.

The Erlenmeyer Flask

The X-Files are closed down and Deep Throat is murdered after directing Mulder to a horrific DNA experiment.

- *Vancouver Drydock Company Ltd./Versatile Pacific Shipyards:* Maryland waterfront. A high-speed car chase ends in a massive diving operation.

Mulder's apartment building, Alexandria, Maryland (The Wellington, 2630 York Avenue).

- *Capilano College:* EMGEN Corporation, Gaithersburg, Maryland. Mulder and Scully investigate the death of Dr. Terrance Allan Berube.
- *The Wellington, 2630 York Avenue:* Alexandria, Maryland. In front of Mulder's apartment building, Deep Throat urges Mulder to continue the investigation. Deep Throat later meets Scully here.
- *Pacific Maco, 1616 Pandora Street:* Zuess Storage, 1616 Pandora Street. Georgetown, Maryland. Mulder discovers tanks filled with alien/human hybrid clones.

Some of the most respected and renowned film directors in the world have lensed footage in British Columbia during the past hundred years. Included among them are Thomas Edison, Dorothy Arzner, Michael Powell, William Castle, Robert Altman, Mike Nichols, Wolfgang Peterson, Jean-Jacques Annaud, Nicholas Roeg, Bob Fosse, John Carpenter, Fred Schepisi, and John Woo.

- *Vanterm Overpass, 300-block Clark Drive:* Georgetown, Maryland. Scully watches from her car as Deep Throat is assassinated and Mulder is dumped from the back of a van.

Season 2

Little Green Men

With the X-Files closed down, Scully is sent back to teach in Quantico and Mulder, stuck with a boring textbook case, entertains himself by retrieving top-secret alien-contact tapes while fixating on the abduction of his sister.

- *Plaza of Nations underground parking:* Watergate Hotel, Washington, D.C. Mulder and Scully meet covertly in a parking garage.
- *Simon Fraser University:* Exterior of FBI Headquarters, Washington, D.C.
- *Seymour Demonstration Forest:* National Astronomy and Ionosphere Centre in Arecibo, Puerto Rico. Mulder retrieves secret alien-contact tapes.
- *Plaza of Nations, B.C. Enterprises Building:* Miami International Airport. Scully dodges government agents before catching a plane to meet Mulder.

The Host

Mulder enlists Scully's help in tracking down a mutant "fluke-man" responsible for a series of grisly murders in the New Jersey sewer system.

- *Lower Lonsdale:* Newark, New Jersey. Mulder arrives to investigate a death in the New Jersey sewer.
- *False Creek, east of Anderson's Restaurant:* Washington Monument. Mulder and Scully meet covertly to discuss the case.
- *Iona Island Sewage Treatment Plant:* Newark County Sewage Processing Plant, New Jersey. The mutant fluke-man is tracked and killed.

Blood

A quiet postal clerk figures prominently in a case that takes Mulder to unassuming Franklin, Pennsylvania, where either poisonous subliminal messages or environmental toxins may be the cause of a series of gruesome murders.

- *Capitol Centre, New Westminster:* Franklin, Pennsylvania, Civic Centre. Ed Funsch kills four people on an elevator.

Franklin Community College (University of British Columbia).

- *Army & Navy Department Store, 502 Columbia Street, New Westminster:* The department store where Ed Funsch gets spooked after seeing a blood-drive banner.
- *Dunlevy Avenue and Powell Street, Vancouver:* The Franklin Community General Hospital bus drops Ed Funsch off near the "college."
- *UBC Main Library and Ladner Clock Tower:* Franklin Community College. Ed Funsch climbs the tower and starts shooting people.

Before being hailed as "the reinvention of television," David Lynch's *Twin Peaks* TV pilot had its premiere at the 1989 Vancouver International Film Festival. Many filmgoers, thinking they were seeing a "real movie," were left perplexed and befuddled by its cliffhanger ending!

Sleepless

Mulder's own sleeplessness parallels the case of a group of Vietnam vets suffering from chronic insomnia and crushing guilt for their part in a Korean village massacre.

- *Vancouver Hospital, 855 West 12th Avenue:* The Grissom Sleep Disorder Centre, Stamford, Connecticut. After Mulder investigates the centre, his new partner, Krycek, meets up with him and voices his disapproval.
- *GM Place:* During their first meeting, Deep Throat's replacement, X, tells Mulder that "the truth is still out there."
- *2 Jays Cafe, 81 West Pender Street:* 2 Jays Cafe, Roslyn, New York. Mulder and Krycek meet with Salvator Mantola, the only survivor of the government's sleep annihilation experiment.
- *Via Rail Station:* Bronx Station. Krycek and Mulder meet neurosurgeon Francis Giorardi while on the train platform. Augustus "Preacher" Cole makes Mulder believe he has been shot.
- *Versatile Pacific Shipyards:* Krycek kills "Preacher" Cole, who he believed was going to shoot him.

Duane Barry

The first of two parts. Mulder is taken into the bizarre fantasy world of a former FBI agent who insists he be taken to the site where aliens once abducted him.

- ***St. George's School, 4175 West 29th Avenue:*** Davis Correctional Treatment Facility. After his close encounter, Duane Barry is committed here.
- ***UBC indoor pool:*** Washington, D.C., pool. Krycek tells Mulder about the hostage situation.
- ***Waterfront Centre, Police Community Service Office, 200 Burrard Street:*** Travel Time Agency, Richmond, Virginia. Mulder meets Duane Barry during the hostage crisis.
- ***Stong's Market, 4560 Dunbar Street:*** After analyzing Duane Barry's implant, Scully goes grocery shopping and scans the implant at a cashier's station.

Ascension

The second of two parts. Mulder doesn't know what or who to believe when Duane Barry tells him that Scully has been abducted by aliens herself and their supervisor reopens the X-Files in apparent frustration.

- ***The Wellington, 2630 York Avenue:*** Alexandria, Maryland. Mulder's apartment building. Mulder listens to Scully's desperate phone message.
- ***1419 Pendrell Street, West End:*** Annapolis, Maryland. Scully's apartment building. After Scully's abduction the street and building are the scene of a massive police investigation.
- ***Simon Fraser University:*** FBI Headquarters, Washington, D.C.

Skyland Mountain, Virginia (Grouse Mountain).

- *Grouse Mountain:* Skyland Mountain, Virginia. Mulder rides the skylift while Barry drives up the mountain with Scully in his car trunk.
- *Robson Square, parking level 2:* Washington, D.C. Krycek meets covertly with the Cigarette Smoking Man.
- *Vancouver Art Gallery:* The office of Senator Richard Matheson. Washington, D.C. X prevents Mulder from visiting the senator.
- *Robson Square:* When Mulder tries to return Scully's necklace to her mother, she replies, "When you find her you give it to her."

Movie star Rita Hayworth got her start in the late thirties by acting opposite Charles Quigley in a pair of back-to-back Victoria-made "quota quickies." Both *Across the Border* and *Convicted* had Hayworth playing a stereotypical damsel in distress.

3

Distraught and lonely, Mulder travels to L.A. and has an affair with the human associate of a group of vampires.

- *Oasis Club, North Vancouver:* Club Tepes, Los Angeles. Mulder meets Kristen.
- *Plaza of Nations, B.C. Enterprises Building:* Ra Restaurant, Los Angeles. After Mulder gets the boot for pulling a Peeping Tom act, Kristen and her cohorts murder another victim.
- *SW Marine Drive, home of Vancouver Canucks' Pavel Bure:* 1533 Malibu Canyon, Los Angeles. Kristen seduces Mulder.

One Breath

The delicate psychic bond between Mulder and Scully becomes a precious lifeline for both of them when Scully is found in a coma.

- *B.C. Children's Hospital, 4480 Oak Street:* Northeast Georgetown Medical Centre, Washington, D.C. After her disappearance, Scully reappears here.
- *Seymour Demonstration Forest, Rice Lake:* While in a coma, Scully dreams she's in a boat on a lake, while Nurse Owens looks on from a wharf.

- *Hotel Vancouver laundry room:* Hospital laundry room. After a government agent steals a vial of Scully's blood, Mulder chases him downstairs. X, after telling Mulder, "You want to see what it takes to find the truth?" shoots the man in the head.

> Oops! Take 5: While filming the feature *First Blood* near the Cleveland Dam at Capilano Canyon, Sylvester Stallone and the film's prop department were startled to discover that a gun arsenal had been stolen from a locked truck. The guns were never recovered, but three years later three men were charged with the theft, only months before the film's *Rambo* sequel was released.

Firewalker

A rescue call from an isolated volcano-research group certain that their leader is a crazed messiah becomes a fight against an infectious, silicon-based fungus organism that lives in the volcano.

- *Seymour Demonstration Forest boneyard:* Mt. Avalon, Cascade Mountain Range.
- *BC Hydro Substation, 1st Avenue and Nanaimo:* The research team's isolated facility.

Red Museum

A New Age church of Wisconsin vegetarians squares off with the local cattle economy when young children begin reappearing after being abducted and experimented upon with dangerous growth hormones.

- *Uncle Herbert's Fish and Chips, 4866 Delta Street, Ladner Village:* Clay's BBQ. Mulder and Scully are dining on ribs when the sheriff's son starts harassing one of the Red Museum disciples outside.
- *Ladner Village, Delta:* Delta Glen, Wisconsin. The Church of the Red Museum disciples have an altercation with the townsfolk.
- *J & L Beef Ltd. 17565 65A Avenue, Surrey:* Delta Glen Meat Packers. The sheriff shoots and kills the "crew-cut man" (the same man who killed Deep Throat in "The Erlenmeyer Flask").

Excelsis Dei

Alzheimer's patients in a convalescent home mysteriously regain their faculties then die and haunt the halls after a Malaysian orderly begins sharing a deceptively innocent herbal remedy with them.

Excelsis Dei Convalescent Home, Worcester, Massachusetts (Riverview Hospital, West Lawn building).

- ***Riverview Hospital:*** Excelsis Dei Convalescent Home, Worcester, Massachusetts. Mulder and Scully investigate the strange goings-on at the convalescent home.

Aubrey

An elderly serial killer's method appears to be back in style when the murderer's psychotic tendencies get genetically passed on to his granddaughter.

- ***Colbrook Road, South Surrey:*** Aubrey, Missouri. The crime scene where the bodies of FBI agents were discovered from a forty-year-old murder.
- ***Queen's Park, New Westminster:*** Lincoln Park, Aubrey. Mulder and Scully speak with Detective B. J. Morrow about her strange dreams regarding the murder.
- ***1st Street and 3rd Avenue, New Westminster:*** Thibedeaux residence, 238 North 54th Street, Edmond, Nebraska. Mulder and Scully speak with a victim who survived Harry Cokely's attack and who is later attacked by Detective B. J. Morrow.

Before the 1980s version of the made-in-Ontario TV series *The Littlest Hobo*, there was a 1960s original shot in Vancouver. Sixty-four episodes, starring Canadian canine "London," were made and syndicated around the world.

Irresistible

A "death fetishist" who collects souvenirs from funeral parlours gets ambitious and starts stealing from the living. His next prize? Agent Scully.

- ***Mountain View Cemetery:*** Minneapolis cemetery. Mulder and Scully investigate the desecration of a grave.
- ***425 Carrall Street:*** Interior of Ficicello Frozen Foods. Don Eddie Pfaster applies for a job.
- ***50-block Hastings Street:*** Minneapolis street. Don Eddie Pfaster picks up a prostitute and takes her back to his apartment.
- ***Simon Fraser University:*** FBI Headquarters, Washington, D.C.
- ***Clairmont Camera Building, North Shore Studios:*** Charles Lindbergh Terminal. Scully returns to Minneapolis where she rents a car and subsequently gets abducted by Pfaster.

Die Hand Die Verletzt

An occult-style murder is the tip of the iceberg when Mulder and Scully investigate a devil-worshipping cult that operates out of a small New Hampshire schoolhouse.

- ***Seymour Demonstration Forest:*** Milford Haven, New Hampshire. Frogs rain down on Scully and Mulder.
- ***Marian School, 7650 Sapperton Avenue, Burnaby:*** Crowley High School, Milford Haven. The site of some very strange and typically X-File events.

Fresh Bones

A North Carolina refugee camp for Haitians is a voodoo hotbed as Mulder and Scully try to ascertain a marine's cause of death.

- ***Ministry of Transport Service Road, Boundary Bay:*** Folkstone, North Carolina. Private McAlpin drives into a tree that holds mysterious voodoo markings.
- ***Versatile Pacific Shipyards:*** Folkstone I.N.S. Processing Center. Mulder chases a young Haitian boy around the refugee holding facility.

- *North Vancouver Cemetery:* Folkstone Municipal Cemetery. Bodies continue to be dug up, including that of Mr. Bovaine by Colonel Wharton.
- *Beneath the Second Narrows Bridge, North Vancouver:* Outside a Folkstone café, Mulder and Scully are warned by Private Dunham about the camp.

Who says film productions only take from the community? For the TV series *Madison*, teenaged volunteers filled Vancouver's Vogue theatre in an episode that featured MuchMusic VJ Erica Ehm. In return for their services, Forefront Productions donated money to the drama departments of the participating students' high schools.

Colony

The first of two parts. The murders of several identical-looking doctors lead Mulder and Scully to an alien bounty hunter who's doing target practice killing off alien-cloned copies of the human original. He's also hunting Mulder's long-lost, alien-abducted sister, who has seemingly been returned to earth.

- *Boundary Bay Airport:* Mulder is choppered to a government base after suffering from "exposure" in the Beaufort Sea near Alaska.
- *Vancouver Hospital, 855 West 12th Avenue:* Woman's Care Family Services, Scranton, Pennsylvania. The site at which the first Gregor clone is murdered.
- *Vancouver Hospital, nurses' residence:* Binghamton, New York, Globe & Mail newspaper offices. Mulder and Scully look for clues to the killer's whereabouts.
- *Simon Fraser University:* FBI Headquarters, Washington, D.C.
- *1419 Pendrell Street, West End*: Annapolis, Maryland. Scully's apartment building. Mulder runs into CIA agent Ambrose Chapel, who later tells them of the Gregor Cloning Project.
- *Celtic Shipyards, 3150 Celtic Street, Southlands:* Germantown, Maryland, 3243 Edmonton Street. Site of the secret cloning factory.
- *Broughton Street, West End:* Dr. Dickens jumps out of his apartment window when Scully, Mulder, and Chapel come to his door.
- *Gastown:* Dr. Dickens is chased by Scully, Mulder, and Chapel through streets and alleys where Scully steps in green goo.
- *Southlands area, south of SW Marine Drive:* Martha's Vineyard, West Tisbury, Massachusetts. The residence of Mulder's father.

The dozens of extras who showed up for work on the Stewart, B.C., set of the feature film *Leaving Normal* were rewarded with a T-shirt that read, "Leaving Normal for Eternity," which was actually the film's original title.

- ***Safeway, Cardero Street at Davie Street:*** Trying to get back to the cloning factory in Germantown without being followed, Scully boards the Davie Street bus at this location. The alien bounty hunter, "the Pilot," is also on the bus.

End Game

The second of two parts. While Mulder learns that his "sister" is actually a clone, he also learns she's still alive somewhere. X tells Mulder where to find the alien bounty hunter.

- ***Lions Gate Travelodge, North Vancouver:*** Vacation Village Motor Lodge. Scully faces down "the Pilot," disguised as Mulder.
- ***Alouette River Bridge, Harris Road, Pitt Meadows:*** Old Memorial Bridge, Bethesda, Maryland. While trying to kill "the Pilot," Mulder exchanges his sister for Scully.
- ***Old School for Girls, 800 Cassiar Street:*** Woman's Health Services Clinic, Rockville, Maryland. Mulder discovers clones of his sister.
- ***Waterfront Park, North Vancouver:*** Kennedy Centre, Washington, D.C. X tells Mulder about the submarine that located the spacecraft.
- ***HMCS* MacKenzie:** Interior of the USS *Allegiance* submarine. The submarine's exterior was built on sound stage 5 at the North Shore Studios.

Fearful Symmetry

Mulder and Scully investigate why the animals at an Idaho zoo (which just happens to be a UFO hot spot) are disappearing.

- ***425 Carrall Street:*** Idaho Mutual Insurance Trust Co. Mulder and Scully investigate a rampaging invisible elephant.
- ***192nd Street and 24th Avenue, Surrey:*** Forty-three miles from Fairfield, Idaho. The zoo's missing elephant encounters a truck and is later found dead on the road.
- ***Stanley Park Zoo:*** Fairfield Zoo, Idaho. Mulder and Scully check out the zoo and its administrators.

- ***1300-block West Pender Street:*** Blake Towers construction site. The zoo's escaped tiger is shot and killed by zookeeper Ed Meecham.
- ***Vancouver Aquarium, whale tank:*** Zoo boardroom. Mulder speaks to zoo director Willa Ambrose about the possibility of the zoo animals being abducted by aliens.

> After the Conservative government privatized Via Rail in 1989, the Gene Hackman train thriller *Narrow Margin* was left without a train. Thankfully, BC Rail threw in an engine, while a collector from Texas supplied the feature film with most of the other cars needed to complete production.

Dod Kalm

"The Philadelphia Experiment" gets the X-Files treatment as Mulder and Scully deal with the case of an abandoned naval destroyer whose survivors are much older than they seem.

- ***Jericho Sailing Centre, 1300 Discovery Street:*** Bethesda Naval Hospital, Maryland. Scully is called in by Mulder to interview the only survivor of a missing naval destroyer.
- ***Jericho Rugby Club:*** The Gildeskal Bar at Port of Tildeska, Norway. Mulder and Scully charter a boat from Henry Trondheim.
- ***HMCS* MacKenzie*:*** The naval destroyer, USS *Ardent*. Mulder and Scully succumb to a rapid-ageing phenomenon.

Humbug

Everyone's a suspect when Mulder and Scully investigate a trailer-park coven of sideshow freaks to solve a nation-wide series of violent murders.

- ***Semiahmoo Park, Marine Drive, White Rock:*** Gibsonville Cemetery, Florida. Site of a very unusual funeral service for Gerald Glazebrook (The Alligator Man).
- ***Marilee's Cafe, 15782 Marine Drive, White Rock:*** Interior of Phil's Diner. Mulder and Scully meet with Sheriff Hamilton to get the low-down on the history of Gibsonville.
- ***First Nation Reserve, White Rock:*** Gulf Breeze Trailer Court. While investigating the bizarre murders in Gibsonville, Mulder and Scully rent sleeping accommodations from an embittered motel manager.

Due to the extensive stunt work in Jackie Chan's *Rumble in the Bronx*, all of the film's supporting actors were actually Vancouver stunt people, who, incidentally, also had *their own* stunt doubles.

- ***Semiahmoo Park, Marine Drive, White Rock:*** While jogging near a stream in Gibsonville, Mulder spots a tattooed man, known as "the Conundrum," eating a raw fish.

The Calusari

Mulder and Scully's investigation into the death of a young boy is complicated by the child's eerie older brother and the Old Country spiritualism of his Romanian grandmother.

- ***Fantasy Garden World, Richmond:*** Lincoln Park, Murray, Virginia. Toddler Teddy Holvey gets killed by a miniature train, which brings Scully and Mulder into the case.
- ***400-block 5th Street, New Westminster:*** The Holvey residence, Arlington, Virginia.
- ***Riverview Hospital:*** St. Matthew's Medical Centre. Charlie Holvey is taken for psychological evaluation following the bizarre ritual performed by his grandmother and her cronies.

F. Emasculata

It looks like a government cover-up when a vicious new plague is hand-delivered to a prison inmate, killing him and infecting his just-escaped cellmates. Ironically, when Scully discovers the disease comes from the same company that is quarantining the prison (and following Mulder as he tracks the escapees), the agents realize *they* have to participate in the cover-up to avoid widespread public panic.

- ***Seymour Demonstration Forest:*** South American jungle. A government researcher discovers, and is infected by, an unknown parasite.
- ***Woodlands School, 9 East Columbia Street, New Westminster:*** Dinwiddie County, Virginia. A federal prison from which two convicts, who are carrying a deadly disease, escape.
- ***Via Rail Terminal:*** The bus station from which escaped prison convicts hit the road.
- ***Deltaport Farmer's Market, 2757 52nd Street, Ladner:*** Gas station. Mulder tracks the escaped convicts, while government officials

land a helicopter and abduct a gas station attendant who has been exposed to the contagion.

Soft Light

Mulder and Scully follow the trail of a researcher in subatomic physics who has just realized that his exposure to radiation has turned his shadow into a flamethrower.

- ***1st Street and 8th Avenue, New Westminster:*** Wysnecki residence, Richmond, Virginia. Mulder and Scully investigate what seems to be spontaneous human combustion.
- ***Via Rail Station:*** Richmond, Virginia, train terminal. Mulder and Scully locate Dr. Chester Banton while Mulder unwittingly supplies X with information on Banton's whereabouts.
- ***Pacific Marine Training Institute, 265 West Esplanade, North Vancouver:*** Polarity Magnetics Building. Mulder and Scully find out about Dr. Banton's work with "dark matter."
- ***Woodlands School, 9 East Columbia Street, New Westminster:*** Interior of the Yaloff Psychiatric Hospital, Piedmont, Virginia. X's attempt to abduct Banton fails.

Train terminal, Richmond, Virginia (Via Rail Station).

Before returning to Vancouver in 1993 to make the big-budget feature *Intersection* with Richard Gere, Sharon Stone appeared in a locally shot and little known science-fiction film called *Beyond the Stars* in 1989. It co-starred Christian Slater and Martin Sheen.

- ***Mountain View Cemetery:*** Scully visits the grave of her former student Kelly Ryan, who was killed when exposed to Banton's shadow.

Our Town

Mulder and Scully investigate the possibility that a biochemical experiment at a poultry plant may have something to do with the mysterious disappearances of the local folk.

- ***Seymour Demonstration Forest:*** County Road A7, Dudley, Arkansas. Woods where George Kerns is beheaded.
- ***Simon Fraser University:*** Exterior of FBI Headquarters, Washington, D.C.
- ***Justice Institute, 715 McBride Avenue, New Westminster:*** The exterior of the Chaco Chicken Factory, Dudley, Arkansas.
- ***Number 4 Road and Finn Road, Richmond:*** Dudley, Arkansas. Empty field where Mulder and Scully investigate foxfire and where Scully is nearly beheaded.

Anasazi

The first of three parts. Mulder's attempts to obtain the coveted "MJ file" (which contains secret, government-held alien information) are complicated by a conspiracy to drug him with LSD and murder his father, as well as the discovery of a long-buried rail car full of "aliens."

- ***Park and Tilford Gardens, North Vancouver:*** Botanic Gardens, Washington, D.C. A computer hacker meets with Mulder and gives him the stolen Defense Department UFO intelligence files.
- ***Southlands area:*** West Tisbury, Martha's Vineyard, Massachusetts. Mulder's father gets a visit from the Cigarette Smoking Man and is later killed by Krycek.
- ***The Wellington, 2630 York Avenue:*** Alexandria, Maryland. Outside Mulder's apartment building. Scully shoots Mulder in the shoulder when he's about to kill Krycek.

- ***Britannia Beach:*** Navajo Reservation, Two Grey Hills, New Mexico. Residence of Albert Hosteen and his family.
- ***Gravel quarry, Quarry Road, Port Coquitlam:*** Navajo Reservation, Two Grey Hills, New Mexico. Mulder is led to a buried train car containing alien corpses.

Season 3

The Blessing Way

The second of three parts. Scully, believing Mulder is dead, returns to Washington, D.C. Here she finds a suspension from the FBI and a strange implant in her neck.

- ***Britannia Beach:*** Navajo Reservation, Two Grey Hills, New Mexico. Scully visits Albert Hosteen to find out what happened to Mulder.
- ***1419 Pendrell Street, West End:*** Annapolis, Maryland. Scully's apartment building. Scully sees FBI assistant director Skinner leaving her building. Later, Skinner pulls up in front of Scully's building and invites her into his car. Later still, Scully's sister enters the building and is shot.
- ***Mountain View Cemetery:*** Garden of Reflection, Parkway Cemetery, Boston, Massachusetts. At the funeral of William Mulder, Scully encounters the Well-Manicured Man.

Scully's apartment building, Annapolis, Maryland (1419 Pendrell Street).

- *Southlands area:* West Tisbury, Martha's Vineyard, Massachusetts. Mulder is waiting in his father's house when his mother returns.

Paper Clip

The third of three parts. With help from conspiracy theorists the Lone Gunmen, Mulder and Scully find an ex-Nazi scientist who directs the agents to an abandoned mine housing a filing system of medical records on millions of people—including Dana Scully and Mulder's missing sister.

> Oops! Take 6: Vancouver has not been kind to actor Michael Dudikoff. While filming an episode of the TV series *Cobra*, Dudikoff ended up with a concussion when a piece of debris hit him in the head after a small explosion. Later, while shooting the feature film *Virtual Assassins*, he wound up with a bruised eye when he was accidentally struck by a stunt person.

- *Southlands Nursery, 6550 Balaclava Street:* The greenhouse where Mulder and Scully question Victor Klemper about his involvement with the U.S. government.
- *B.C. Museum of Mining, Britannia Beach:* Rural West Virginia. Mulder and Scully visit a secret government facility where they find thousands of medical files, and have a "close encounter."
- *Britannia Beach, The Tea Shoppe:* Charlotte's Diner, Craiger, Maryland. Skinner meets with Mulder and Scully.
- *The Lynnwood Inn, 1515 Barrow Street, North Vancouver:* Southeast Washington, D.C. Krycek is almost killed when the car he's riding in explodes.

D.P.O.

Mulder and Scully have to keep at arm's length when dealing with a socially stunted but electrified video arcade jockey who has the power to strike down those around him when crossed.

- *Capilano Village, Marine Drive and Fell Avenue, North Vancouver:* Connerville, Oklahoma. The video arcade where Darren Peter Oswald kills Jack Hammond using "lightning."
- *Ministry of Transport service road, Boundary Bay:* Rural road intersection. Darren Oswald and his pal Zero create a traffic accident.

- *Measurex Devron Inc., 500 Brooksbank Avenue, North Vancouver:* Felton Community Hospital. Mulder investigates the link between Darren Oswald and his boss's wife, which leads to an electrifying conclusion.

> Canada's first permanent movie theatre was built in 1902 at 42 West Cordova Street in Gastown. The Edison Electric played all the great films of the day but only lasted four years. The building was taken over by a clothing retailer then demolished in 1908, and today the Army & Navy Department Store stands on the site.

Clyde Bruckman's Final Repose

Mulder and Scully call on a mild-mannered psychic to help solve a series of murders in which the victims were fortunetellers and the killer himself may be psychic.

- *Seymour Demonstration Forest, Rice Lake:* Minneapolis/St. Paul. Following up on a tip from Clyde Bruckman, Mulder and Scully discover a victim in a lake, and a propane tank that looks like a "fat little white Nazi stormtrooper." Later they find another victim in the woods.
- *3500-block Commercial Drive:* Mulder and Scully locate another murder victim inside a crystal store.

The List

The case for reincarnation gets a boost when Mulder and Scully receive a courtesy call from a killer who has just been executed.

- *Riverview Hospital:* Florida State Prison. Mulder and Scully investigate the strange goings-on of, and bizarre murders by, a just-executed death-row inmate.

2 Shy

When lonely, overweight women who frequent Internet chat lines keep ending up liquefied, Mulder and Scully have to find the concrete evidence that will lead them to the oddball killer.

- *Versatile Pacific Shipyards:* Cleveland waterfront. The first victim of Virgil Incanto is found dead in her car. Her body fat has been sucked

Before starting Cineplex-Odeon Cinemas, and later becoming a theatre mogul with hits such as *Kiss of the Spider Woman* and *Showboat*, Canada's Garth Drabinsky produced the comedy feature *Losin' It* (featuring one of the first appearances by Shelley Long and Tom Cruise) and the made-in-Vancouver thriller *The Changeling*. He also ran the tiny Bay Cinema (now known as the Starlight) on Denman Street in Vancouver's West End.

out, leaving the corpse looking like a mummy wrapped in goo.

- *2649 Quebec Street:* Virgil Incanto's building. Most people who enter his apartment don't come out alive.
- *Beneath the north end of the Granville Street Bridge:* Virgil Incanto picks up a prostitute under the bridge and, after a struggle, relieves her of her body fat.

The Walk

Mulder and Scully have to play psychiatrist as well as FBI agent when a poltergeist haunts the increasingly suicidal soldiers at a veterans' hospital.

- *Vancouver Hospital, 855 West 12th Avenue:* Army hospital psychiatric ward. Fort Evanston, Maryland. Mulder and Scully investigate a botched suicide attempt.
- *Justice Institute, 715 McBride Avenue, New Westminster:* The army hospital swimming pool. Site of a murder by a ghostly disembodied figure.

Oubliette

When a teenaged girl is kidnapped by a psychotic, Mulder turns for help to another young woman—one who appears to have been kidnapped by the same man before.

- *Argyle Secondary School, 1131 Frederick Road, North Vancouver:* Valley Woods High School, Seattle, Washington. While helping with school photographs, Carl Wade sees his teenaged victim.
- *B.C. Children's Hospital:* University Medical Centre. Lucy Householder is treated after collapsing at a diner.
- *Normanna Rest Home, 7979 12th Avenue, Burnaby:* Bright Angel Halfway House. Lucy stays here after leaving the hospital.

- *Mount Seymour Ranger's Station:* Carl Wade's house near the woods in Easton, Washington.
- *100-block 1st Street East and Lower Lonsdale, North Vancouver:* Easton, Washington. Mulder and Scully pursue Carl Wade back to his house and into the woods.

Vancouver seems to be a great place to catch a glimpse of your favourite *Star Trek* actor. Alumni from the popular science-fiction TV series who have filmed projects in the city include Patrick Stewart *(Smart Alec)*, Leonard Nimoy and Brent Spiner *(The Outer Limits)*, Jonathan Frakes *(University Hospital)*, William Shatner *(Secrets of a Married Man and The Prisoner of Zenda Inc.)*, Nichelle Nichols *(Captain Zoom)*, Denise Crosby *(Max)*, and Rene Auberjonois *(McCabe and Mrs. Miller)*. Vancouver-born James Doohan even took part in a locally produced game show.

Nisei

The first of two parts. Mulder uncovers a videotape that documents an actual "alien autopsy," much to the chagrin of Big Brother.

- *Hycroft Mansion:* The Japanese Embassy, where a diplomat gets murdered.
- *Centennial Pier, 555 Centennial Road:* U.S. Coastguard Headquarters, Newport News, Virginia. Mulder speaks with coastguard captain about the ship *Talapus*.
- *Vancouver Drydock Company Ltd. and Versatile Pacific Shipyards:* U.S. Coastguard Headquarters. Mulder is chased off the *Talapus* and jumps into the water, later emerging to peek inside a warehouse where he sees what he believes to be a UFO.
- *North Shore Railyard:* The government's underground railroad at Quinnimont, West Virginia. Mulder witnesses what he believes to be an E.B.E. escorted onto train car #82517.
- *BC Rail Passenger Station, 1131 1st Street, North Vancouver:* The North East Rail Station, where a train carrying mysterious cargo, and bound for Vancouver, B.C., departs.
- *Vancouver Art Gallery:* Office of Senator Richard Matheson, Washington, D.C. Mulder asks for advice on how to proceed on the case.

Before making such on-the-edge thrillers as *The Krays* and *Romeo Is Bleeding*, British director Peter Medak helmed the Genie Award-winning made-in-Vancouver horror film *The Changeling*.

- ***Simon Fraser University:*** Exterior of FBI Headquarters, Washington, D.C.

731

The second of two parts. The government's alien cover-up continues as Mulder finds more evidence of extra-terrestrial life and Scully has to trust a government henchman to save her partner.

- ***Seymour Demonstration Forest boneyard:*** Perkey, West Virginia. After shooting dozens of "alien" looking creatures, the military dumps them in a mass grave.
- ***Sea to Sky Corridor:*** Mulder rides on top of the North East Rail train bound for Vancouver.
- ***Seymour Demonstration Forest:*** Hansen's Disease Research Facility, Perkey, West Virginia. Scully encounters a leper colony.
- ***Porteau Cove, Sea to Sky Highway:*** X comes to Mulder's rescue just before the train car he is trapped in explodes.

Revelations

While the agents try to protect a special young boy from a maniac who is murdering religious zealots, Mulder's patience is tested and Scully questions her faith.

- ***St. Anselm's Church, University Boulevard, UBC:*** First Church of Redemption, Waynesburg, Pennsylvania. After giving a sermon, Reverend Finley is murdered by Simon Gates.
- ***Ridgeway Elementary School, 420 East 8th Avenue, North Vancouver:*** Ridgeway Elementary School, Loveland, Ohio. Kevin Carter displays signs of stigmata as his hands bleed while doing a mathematics problem.
- ***Westward Inn, 19650 Fraser Highway, Langley:*** Westward Inn, Loveland, Ohio. Mulder and Scully bring Kevin here after his mother is killed. Simon Gates abducts him from the motel room's bathroom.
- ***BFI Recycling Systems, 5324 Thorne Street, Burnaby:*** 21st Century Recycling Plant, Jerusalem, Ohio. Scully tracks down Kevin to

Simon Gates's recycling plant, where Gates gets killed in a paper mulcher.

War of the Coprophages

While visiting a small town, Mulder discovers there's more to the local cockroach population than meets the eye.

- *Seymour Demonstration Forest:* Miller's Grove, Massachusetts. Mulder is parked in his car, contemplating the universe, when the local sheriff arrives.
- *6351 Pearkes Drive, Terra Nova, Richmond:* The cockroach house where Mulder meets Dr. Bambi Berenbaum.
- *Crane Manufacturing, 225 North Road, Burnaby:* Interior of Alt Fuels Inc. Mulder is attacked by the bugged-out Dr. Jeff Eckerle, who fires his gun and sets off an explosion.
- *Cannery Warehouse, 6741 Caribou Road, Burnaby:* Exterior of Alt Fuels Inc. Mulder and Scully escape from the building just before the explosion.

> During the 1972 Academy Awards, best actress and best supporting actress nominations went to women starring in Vancouver-made movies: Julie Christie in *McCabe and Mrs. Miller*, and Ann-Margret in *Carnal Knowledge*. Unfortunately, neither actress won and this situation hasn't occurred since.

Syzygy

A series of satanic murders brings Mulder and Scully to a small town, where Mulder believes a bizarre astrological phenomenon may be responsible for the deaths.

- *Seymour Demonstration Forest:* Comity woods, Caryl County. Teenager Jay DeBoon gives a eulogy for a deceased friend and later gets killed by a pair of high school girls.
- *Ministry of Transport Service Road, Boundary Bay:* Comity city limits. Mulder and Scully get disoriented as they enter Comity, "the perfect harmony city."
- *Windsor Secondary School, 931 Broadview Drive, North Vancouver:* Grover Cleveland Alexander High School. While playing basketball in the gymnasium, another student is killed.
- *Ladner:* The Comity townsfolk hysterically dig up a field they believe is a mass grave.

The very first Vancouverite to be nominated for an Academy Award was John Ireland for his supporting role in the 1949 Oscar-winning film *All the King's Men*. The only local actors since then to be up for Oscar were Chief Dan George for the 1970 western *Little Big Man*, Meg Tilly for the 1985 film *Agnes of God*, and her sister Jennifer Tilly for the 1994 Woody Allen comedy, *Bullets over Broadway*. All were nominated in the supporting category.

- ***Atlas Restaurant, 5011 48th Avenue, Ladner:*** Terri Roberts and Margi Kleinjan try to pick up Scott Williams at the local diner.

Grotesque

Could demonic possession be the key to a string of copycat serial killings? Mulder's former mentor enlists his and Scully's help to find out.

- ***Heritage Hall, 3102 Main Street:*** George Washington University, Washington, D.C. After drawing a gargoyle's portrait at a university extension class, John Mostow murders the class model in a back alley.
- ***B.C. Rehabilitation GF Strong Centre, 4255 Laurel Street:*** D.C. Correctional Compound, Lorton, Virginia. Mulder and Scully question John Mostow after his incarceration.
- ***8355 Wiggins Road, Burnaby:*** 1222 South Dakota Street, Washington, D.C. Mulder discovers gargoyle sculptures at John Mostow's studio. Later he fights with Agent Patterson on the building's roof.

Piper Maru

The first of two parts. After a boatload of French sailors shows up with inexplicable radiation burns, Mulder and Scully's investigation leads them to yet another mysterious government conspiracy.

- ***Ballantyne Pier, north foot of Heatley Street:*** U.S. Naval Station, San Diego. Mulder and Scully examine the *Piper Maru*.
- ***Vancouver Detachment, CFB Chilliwack at Jericho, 4th Avenue and Highbury Street:*** Miramar Naval Air Station, California. After discovering that a P51 Mustang is sitting at the bottom of the ocean, Scully visits Commander Johansen looking for answers.

Hong Kong restaurant (Ho Ho Chop Suey, Chinatown).

- ***Beneath the Second Narrows Bridge, north side:*** 3702 Medlock Street, San Francisco. Mulder visits the Kallenchuk Salvage Brokers office.
- ***Ballantyne Pier, Cruise Ship Facility:*** San Francisco International Airport. Mulder catches a flight to Hong Kong.
- ***The Meatmarket Restaurant, 1 West Cordova Street, Gastown:*** Washington, D.C. Assistant Director Skinner is threatened by government security officials and later shot.
- ***Ho Ho Chop Suey, 100 East Pender Street, Chinatown:*** Mulder tracks down Jeraldine Kallenchuk in a Hong Kong restaurant.
- ***Ballantyne Pier, Cruise Ship Facility:*** Hong Kong Airport. Mulder tracks down Krycek.

Apocrypha

The second of two parts. While Scully investigates the shooting of Assistant Director Skinner, Mulder gets closer to uncovering a government conspiracy.

- ***Mount St. Joseph's Hospital, 3080 Prince Edward Street:*** Northeast Georgetown Medical Centre, Washington, D.C. After Skinner's shooting, Scully speaks with him about his would-be assassin.

While visiting Vancouver in 1994 for the Molson Indy, superstar Paul Newman surprised a young bride-to-be with a kiss at the popular Robson Street eatery CinCin.

- ***Highway 17 overpass, Delta:*** County Road 512, Maryland. Krycek and Mulder are run off the road by a pair of shady G-men.
- *Robson Square*: Rockville, Maryland. The Lone Gunmen skate around the Capitol Ice Rink before retrieving a package for Mulder.
- ***Howe Street at Robson Street:*** The Lone Gunmen give Mulder the DAT package and discover it's empty.
- ***Stanley Park, near Lord Stanley Statue:*** Central Park, New York City. Mulder meets with the Well-Manicured Man to discuss Krycek and the government cover-up.
- ***355 Burrard Street:*** While Scully rides in an ambulance with A.D. Skinner, Luis Cardinale attempts to kill them. Scully pursues Cardinale down the street on foot.
- ***Boundary Bay:*** Black Crow, North Dakota. Mulder and Scully look for a UFO in Black Crow's abandoned missile silos.
- ***Stanley Park:*** Mulder visits Scully at the grave of her sister, Melissa.

Pusher

Is it suicide or is it murder? Mulder and Scully help investigate the case of a man who has the ability to "will" people to death.

- ***False Creek Grocer, 760 West 6th Avenue:*** Mt. Foodmore Supermarket, Loudon County, Virginia. The FBI tracks down Robert Modell (a.k.a. Pusher) while on his weekly shopping excursion.
- ***Gastown parking lot:*** Beltway Commuter Lot, Falls Church, Virginia. Mulder and Scully monitor pay phones hoping to hear from "Pusher."
- ***Takaya Golf Centre, 700 Apex Road, North Vancouver:*** Tee Totaller's Golf Driving Range & Pro Shop. After driving some golf balls, Modell forces Agent Collins to set himself on fire.
- ***Granville Square, north foot of Granville Street:*** FBI Headquarters lobby. Modell gains access to the department's computer records system by making those around him believe his hand-written security pass is real.

Teso Dos Bichos

After an ancient artifact is brought back to the United States from South America, Mulder and Scully are called in to find out why the museum's employees are being murdered.

- *Seymour Demonstration Forest:* Teso Dos Bichos excavation site. Ecuadorean Highlands, South America. An American archaeologist digs up something he shouldn't have!
- *Riverview Hospital:* Boston Museum of Natural History. Mulder and Scully investigate the death of a museum proprietor and later struggle to fend off savage cats and rats.

> Few are aware of it, but the film biz is one of the most environmentally conscious industries around. Sets, props, and costumes are constantly being recycled. In fact, on the made-in-B.C. feature *Little Women*, actor Mar Andersons was outfitted in the same grey suit that Gary Oldman wore in *Bram Stoker's Dracula.*

Hell Money

Mulder and Scully enlist the help of a reluctant Asian-American police officer when investigating a series of strange murders in San Francisco's Chinatown.

- *Chinatown:* Chinatown, San Francisco, California. Mulder and Scully investigate the mysterious burning death of a young Chinese man.
- *Keefer Rooms Building, 200-block Keefer Street, Chinatown:* Exterior of apartment building where Mulder, Scully, and Detective Chao question Mr. Hsin about the carpet he laid. Later, the "hard-faced man" pays Mr. Hsin a threatening visit.
- *Wise Social Club, 1882 Adanac Street:* Chinatown Hall where hopeful immigrants take part in a life-and-death "lottery."
- *Seymour Demonstration Forest:* Highland Park Cemetery. Mulder discovers a body in an open grave.
- *100 East Pender Street, Chinatown:* Chinatown Hall exterior entrance. Mulder and Scully follow Detective Chao inside and discover the "lottery."

Expo 86 is long gone, but the memories of its pavilions live on in the Disney television miniseries *Earth Star Voyager*. Several of the Expo venues were used as locations for the futuristic space odyssey, including the popular Soviet Union Pavilion and Expo Centre (now Science World).

Jose Chung's *From Outer Space*

While researching a book on alien abductions, a famous writer discovers multiple versions of the same bizarre story.

- *Seymour Demonstration Forest:* Klass County, Washington. The site of Chrissy and Harold's "alien abduction," Roky Orikensen's witnessing of the "abduction," Mulder and Scully's recovery of a "bleepin' dead alien body," Mulder's roadside encounter with naked Lt. Jack Schaffer, and the Air Force's top-secret-project crash site.
- *The Ovaltine Cafe, 251 East Hastings Street:* Klass County Diner. Mulder speaks with Jack Schaffer about the "alien abduction" and later questions the diner's cook while ordering multiple servings of sweet potato pie.

Avatar

Mulder and Scully put their investigative technique into overdrive when Assistant Director Skinner is accused of murdering a prostitute.

- *Georgia Hotel, 801 West Georgia Street:* Chesapeake Lounge, Ambassador Hotel, Washington, D.C. While having a drink at a local bar, A.D. Skinner meets up with prostitute Corina Sayles. Later, in the hotel, he kills the man responsible for her murder.
- *Seymour Street at Robson:* While driving her car through the rain, Scully speaks on the phone with Mulder about Skinner's situation.
- *Viva Tower, 828 Drake Street:* 1223 Hanover Street, Georgetown. Mulder and Scully visit Lorraine Kellaher at her apartment, where she is later found dead.
- *626 Bute Street at Melville:* Second District Police Station. After confronting Skinner on the police station steps, Mulder and Scully encounter Mrs. Skinner.
- *The Elbow Room Cafe, 560 Davie Street:* Mulder and Scully speak with Judy Fairly about the government employee who's trying to frame Skinner.

Quagmire

A series of missing persons reports brings Mulder and Scully to a small town where there might be a sea monster on the loose.

- ***Pitt Lake, Pitt Meadows:*** Strikers Cove, Henvelman's Lake, Blue Ridge Mountains, Georgia. Mulder and Scully investigate the disappearance of government researcher Dr. Bailey.
- ***Seymour Demonstration Forest, Rice Lake:*** Mulder and Scully try to persuade local police to close Henvelman's Lake after there are two more unexplained deaths.
- ***Buntzen Lake, Port Coquitlam:*** Strikers Cove, Henvelman's Lake. Dr. Farraday is attacked by what turns out to be an alligator. Before it can make Mulder its next victim, he shoots and kills it.

Stan Lee, the creator of *The Incredible Hulk* and many other Marvel comics characters, made a cameo appearance as a juror in the made-for-TV movie *The Trial of the Incredible Hulk*. Lee was so taken with Vancouver that he returned in 1996 to film the TV pilot *I, Werewolf*.

Wetwired

In what may be a government-sanctioned TV mind-control experiment, couch potatoes start acting out violently while Scully succumbs to paranoid delusions. Mulder naturally explores the case's conspiracy angle.

- ***Gastown:*** Washington, D.C. Mulder meets with an associate of X's and is given a newspaper clipping.
- ***2400 Court Motel, 2400 Kingsway:*** The Court Motel, Braddock Heights, Maryland. While viewing murder suspect Patnik's video collection, Scully is influenced by one of the tape's insidious mind-control properties. Later she suffers from paranoid delusions and disappears.
- ***1st Avenue at Highbury Street:*** Braddock Heights, Maryland. After Mulder chases a cable technician down the street, he climbs a power pole and discovers what he thinks is a cable trapper-scrambler device.
- ***Victory Square alley, Gastown:*** Washington, D.C., alley. X meets with The Cigarette Smoking Man to discuss his assignment and Mulder's mysterious informant.

Talitha Cumi

The first of two parts. The search for a mysterious man who possesses the power to heal brings Mulder and Scully closer to the truth about the existence of alien life on earth.

- *A&W Restaurant, 6535 Kingsway, Burnaby:* Arlington, Virginia. With the touch of his hand, Jeremiah Smith heals a gunman and his victims after a shooting incident at the K Brothers fast food restaurant.
- *White Rock:* Quonochontaug, Rhode Island. Mulder's mother meets with the Cigarette Smoking Man at the Mulders' old beach house. Later, Mulder encounters X.
- *Riverview Hospital:* The feds lock up Jeremiah Smith in a facility where the Cigarette Smoking Man speaks with him about "the project."
- *Granville Square, north foot of Granville Street:* FBI Headquarters lobby. Jeremiah Smith turns himself in to Scully and the FBI.
- *Vancouver City Hall:* Social Security Administration, Washington, D.C. Jeremiah Smith escapes from Mulder and Scully as they escort him through the building's lobby.
- **Woodward's Building Parkade:** After refusing to give up the alien weapon found in his mother's summer house, Mulder fights with X.
- **Tolko Industries, 200 Bridge Street, North Vancouver:** Bon Mill Road off I-95. Mulder, Scully, and Jeremiah Smith rendezvous at a wood mill.

Social Security Administration, Washington, D.C. (Vancouver City Hall).

CELEBRITY HOT SPOTS

After the spotlights have dimmed and the cameras stop rolling, many stars come out to play after a long day of shooting. For some, this means enjoying dinner in a nice restaurant, relaxing in a laid-back lounge, or even working out at the local gym.

If you've got a keen eye and a little patience, chances are you could spot your favourite celebrity at one of these places. There are no rules about where and when they will show up, but many productions don't film on Sundays so Saturday nights are a good bet for star-gazing.

Proper etiquette is a must if you're going to ask for an autograph. Never approach people while they are eating, and when the opportunity to speak with a celebrity presents itself be courteous, kind, and never say you prefer their co-star to them.

The locations included in this section are by no means the only places to run into visiting celebrities, but they are spotted here the most often.

The Beijing

865 Hornby Street (604-688-7788)

When the craving for Chinese food hits, celebrities flock to The Beijing. You won't find fancy decor or candlelight at this downtown Asian eatery, but what you *will* find is, arguably, the best oriental seafood in the city. Arrive early to claim a table, but take your time once you've been seated because many stars don't come out until later. Dinner for two will set you back a reasonable sixty dollars.

Some of the Beijing's more famous diners have included Roger Moore, Jane Seymour, Donny Osmond, Olivia Newton-John, John Travolta, Charles Durning, and Lloyd Bridges.

Chameleon Urban Lounge

The Georgia Hotel, 801 West Georgia Street (604-669-0806)

This hip but still cosy nightspot downstairs in the Georgia Hotel is the "in" place downtown to listen to an eclectic blend of jazz, a point not lost on the entertainment industry. "Wrap parties" are often held here, and the bar has been featured in many music videos.

When he's visiting Vancouver, Harry Connick, Jr. drops round for drinks and sometimes surprises patrons by jamming onstage unannounced. Regulars include Rae Dawn Chong, David Duchovny, John Rhys-Davies, The Bare Naked Ladies, and "Elvis."

CinCin Ristorante

1154 Robson Street (604-688-7338)

Just around the corner from the Sutton Place Hotel is CinCin, a Mediterranean-style restaurant very popular with locals and visiting celebrities for its open kitchen, wood-fired oven, award-winning wine list, and delectable desserts. Dinner for two runs about a hundred dollars.

CinCin's clientele includes Robin Williams, who once treated former prime minister Pierre Trudeau to an impromptu stand-up routine at his table during dessert. Other famous folks who've shown up are Charlton Heston, Sidney Poitier, Linda Fiorentino, Tom Selleck, Laura Dern, k.d. lang, and O.J. Simpson prosecutor Marcia Clark.

The Coast Plaza at Stanley Park

1733 Comox Street (604-688-7711)

Long before Johnny Depp was kicked out of The Mark Hotel in New York City, he was ejected from the Coast Plaza for throwing a tantrum. This minor skirmish aside, many entertainers still make the Coast Plaza their hotel of choice while visiting Vancouver. Celebrities can sometimes be seen dining at the hotel's Brassier Restaurant. Sylvester Stallone, Dan Aykroyd, Jeff Goldblum, Christine Lahti, Farrah Fawcett, Kris Kristofferson, Mickey Rooney, and Joey Lawrence have all spent time at the Coast Plaza.

Fitness World

1214 Howe Street (604-681-3232)

If the prospect of sweating on the Lifecycle beside the likes of Jean-Claude Van Damme gets your blood pumping a little faster, you might want to check out Fitness World at the corner of Davie and Howe

Streets. Many stars based in downtown hotels tend to work out here and Fitness World has a "Wall of Fame" near the reception desk to prove it. Among those who've taken advantage of the gym's facilities are Michael Jordan, Ringo Starr, Gloria Estefan, and, yes, Jean-Claude Van Damme.

GM Place

800 Griffiths Way (604-899-7400)

Next door to B.C. Place Stadium is what has affectionately become known as "The Garage," home to the NHL's Vancouver Canucks and the NBA's Vancouver Grizzlies.

Most celebrities seem to show up for basketball games, and one of the keenest fans is former Princeton benchwarmer and *X-Files* FBI agent, David Duchovny. He's often sighted near centre court cheering on the home team. Tom Arnold, Linda Carter, Edward James Olmos, and Bryan Adams have all been spotted courtside.

The Hotel Vancouver

900 West Georgia Street (604-684-3131)

The Hotel Vancouver is one of the city's oldest landmarks and one of its most luxurious hotels. Visiting entertainers can sometimes be seen relaxing in the newly refurbished lounge or enjoying a meal at Griffin's Restaurant.

Every October the hotel hosts the Vancouver International Film Festival, an undeniably excellent place for star-gazing. Among the festival guests who have attended in past years are Shirley MacLaine, Kyle MacLachlan, Rutger Hauer, and Robert Downey, Sr.

Hy's Encore

637 Hornby Street (604-683-7671)

A Vancouver institution, Hy's Encore was once *the* place to spot the world's brightest stars. The likes of Bette Davis, Marlene Dietrich, Jack Benny, Vincent Price, Gary Cooper, and Phyllis Diller were all regulars.

Today, the sophisticated steak house caters more to media hounds, business types, and politicians. Still, for around seventy-five dollars, two people can have an enjoyable dinner and soak up Hy's show-biz history. Some of the senior staff may even treat you to a story about the good old days.

Il Giardino di Umberto

1382 Hornby Street (604-669-2422)

Famous types from far and wide can't resist Umberto Menghi's stylish Tuscan restaurant, where the service is gracious, the atmosphere inviting, and most of all the food impeccable. Dinner for two is around a hundred dollars.

Luciano Pavarotti makes Il Giardino a must whenever he's in Vancouver, as do Anthony Quinn, Sharon Stone, Isabella Rossellini, Sean Connery, and many others who appreciate Umberto's hospitality.

After dining on pasta, Billy Joel even went so far as to ask the famous restaurateur for *his* autograph when purchasing an Umberto cookbook.

Joe Fortes Seafood House

777 Thurlow Street (604-669-1940)

Joe Fortes has been serving up seafood to Vancouver's young and eligible for more than a decade. Its mahogany, brass, and palm decor are complemented by nightly piano music and jazz on Sundays. Dinner for two runs under a hundred dollars.

NBA and NHL stars are among the seafood house's most frequent celebrity diners. Other famous faces: Uma Thurman, Jonathan Frakes, Faye Dunaway, and Rob Schneider.

Le Crocodile

100-909 Burrard Street (604-669-4298)

Le Crocodile is considered one of Vancouver's best French bistros and offers simple yet sophisticated cuisine. Dinner for two is around seventy-five dollars.

Famous folks are always being spotted at Le Crocodile. Those who have visited Michel Jacob's kitchen range from Canadian political leaders such as Jean Chrétien, Kim Campbell, John Turner, and Lucien Bouchard to actors Pierce Brosnan, Tyne Daly, Delta Burke, and Glenn Close.

Mangiamo Ristorante

1116 Mainland Street (604-687-1116)

There's something for everyone at Ken Bogas's busy Italian eatery in Yaletown, including "spaghetti with tomato-basil sauce that Umberto taught Ken how to make" (Menghi is Bogas's brother-in-law). It's classy and urban and valet parking is offered (a must in this part of town). Dinner for two is about a hundred dollars.

Many regulars include NBA and NHL players who visit the area before and after their games. Pavel Bure and the Vancouver Canucks are frequent guests. Among the actor regulars are D. B. Sweeney, Adrian Paul, Jim Byrnes, Sam Elliott, and the crews of *The X-Files, The Outer Limits,* and *Sliders*.

The Molson Indy Vancouver

Concord Pacific Place (604-280-INDY)

Since 1990, Vancouver's fastest three days of the year have been at The Molson Indy. Every Labour Day weekend the city hosts the high-speed event that sees the world's top race car drivers compete on the streets near False Creek. Reserved seating and VIP entertainment options are available on an individual basis.

Thousands of people flock to the city for this event, and celebrities are no different. Watch for the likes of Paul Newman or Tom Cruise to show up.

Pacific Palisades Hotel

1277 Robson Street (604-688-0461)

Found right in the middle of dynamic Robson Street, the Pacific Palisades was one of Vancouver's first hotels to capture the imaginations of Hollywood jet-setters. Today, the business-friendly facility caters mostly to behind-the-scenes film people, but rising stars can still be spotted if you keep on your toes!

Visit the hotel's lower lobby, where a display case boasts the names of all the celebrities who've checked in. Some of those celebrated wayfarers have included Bob Hope, Liza Minnelli, Dennis Hopper, Charles Bronson, Stockard Channing, Jay Leno, Val Kilmer, Cybill Shepherd, Max von Sydow, and The Village People.

Pan Pacific Hotel

300-999 Canada Place (604-662-8111)

This luxury hotel opened for Expo 86 and has been very popular with visiting dignitaries and entertainers ever since.

Situated atop a pier at Canada Harbour Place, it has access to a cruise ship terminal, the Vancouver Trade & Convention Centre, and several restaurants, including the popular Five Sails. Some celebrities who have been sighted here include Elizabeth Taylor, Sean Connery, Harrison Ford, Robin Williams, and Leslie Nielsen.

Star Limousine Service

501-1015 Burrard Street (604-685-5600 or toll free, 1-800-803-9222)

If there's one rule about stardom it is that one does not drive, one is *chauffeured*. For many stars their service of choice is Star Limousine. Each stretch limo is equipped with phones, TVs, and VCRs, so it's easy to see why the company motto is "comfort, security, and satisfaction."

Some of the biggest movie stars in the business have been driven by Star Limousine, *so* big in fact that we can't even mention any names. Just keep your eyes peeled when you see the STAR licence plate. Private sightseeing tours around the Lower Mainland, Whistler, and Victoria are available upon request.

Sutton Place Hotel

845 Burrard Street (604-682-5511)

Voted by the people of Vancouver as "the best hotel in the city" (QM/FM Radio, May 1995), this elegant, European-style hotel offers many exclusive arts and entertainment packages as well as fine dining and a unique chocolate buffet.

The Sutton Place has been featured in such productions as *Bird on a Wire, Trial of the Incredible Hulk, 21 Jumpstreet,* and *Wiseguy,* and caters to more celebrities than any other hotel in town. Showbiz folk can almost always be spotted in the Gerard Lounge. Jean-Claude Van Damme, Shirley MacLaine, Winona Ryder, Terence Stamp, Tom Arnold, Sean Astin, and Michael Chiklis have all called the hotel home.

The Teahouse at Ferguson Point

7501 Stanley Park Drive (604-669-3281)

The Teahouse Restaurant has been a Vancouver landmark since before the Second World War when the building was used as officers' barracks. Today its intimate garden setting at Ferguson Point is a beautiful spot to enjoy dinner, lunch, and weekend brunches. French country cooking is its specialty, and dinner for two can run about a hundred dollars.

Robert De Niro (who often shows up for Sunday brunch when he's in town) and Kurt Russell and Goldie Hawn are Teahouse regulars. Others have included Kirstie Alley, Pam Dawber, Rod Steiger, Peter Strauss, and Mark Harmon.

Tojo's

202-777 West Broadway (604-872-8050)

When it comes to authentic Japanese cuisine, nobody can touch Tojo Hidekazu. His innovative, traditionally prepared food speaks for itself, and dozens of wall-mounted celebrity autographs and awards attest to the restaurant's excellence. Dinner for two will set you back about a hundred dollars.

The jovial Chef Tojo is considered a celebrity in his own right, and if you ask, he'll let you thumb through his personal photo album of famous diners (which features Harrison Ford and Robin Williams).

"Simply everyone comes here," says Tojo, whose list of regulars includes William Shatner, Henry Winkler, Adrian Paul, D. B. Sweeney, Jeff Goldblum, Tom Selleck, Rhea Perlman, Sara MacLachlan, Arrowsmith, Bryan Adams, and John Bon Jovi.

Yaletown Brewing Co.

215-1110 Hamilton Street (604-681-2739)

This unique restaurant/pub/brewery caters to a younger crowd with a taste for Italian. There's a large bar with a great selection of ale, and plenty of pool tables in the back room. Dinner for two runs about sixty dollars, depending on how much you drink.

NHL hockey players, many of whom come here to unwind after a game at GM Place, are Yaletown Brewing Co. habitués. Other notable diners and drinkers are Adam Sandler, Denis Leary, Lindsay Wagner, and Tori Spelling.

CINESTUFF

For as long as Vancouver has had a film industry, it has also had a variety of unique retail outlets and theatres that cater to casual and die-hard film aficionados. If memorabilia-collecting or movie-watching are your passions then this assortment of cinema-related stuff will be right up your alley. A selection of locally related on-line film services are also included for those plugged into the Internet.

Admit One–World of Animation

1140 Robson Street (604-685-2728)

A fun store that combines the best of cartoon art galleries with collectable "character apparel" and movie memorabilia. Hats, shirts, and jackets are all emblazoned with studio logos, and rare animation cel art is ready to hang on your wall.

Backstage

432 West Pender Street (604-331-0675)

This quirky hole-in-the-wall shop on West Pender is crammed with movie, television, and music paraphernalia. Hollywood nostalgia abounds and includes vintage film posters, movie magazines, and celebrity autographs. A truly great find for collectors.

Biz Books

136 East Cordova (604-669-6431)

Located in the Vancouver Performing Arts Centre, this is Vancouver's only resource centre dedicated to theatre, film, and television. At Biz, both the novice and the professional can pick up the latest industry periodicals, manuals, plays, and software, surf the net, scan the call board, and enjoy a steaming cup of java.

Captain Video

986 Denman Street (604-682-4044)

Captain Video is one of the best specialty rental outlets in the city and has an extensive selection of laser discs and VHS tapes, including those hard-to-find titles the big stores just don't carry. Recommended for discerning cinephiles.

The Cinémathèque

1131 Howe Street (twenty-four-hour film information: 604-688-3456)

If you are dedicated to the understanding and exhibition of Canadian and world cinema, the Cinémathèque is for you. From Eisenstein's *Battleship Potemkin* to De Sica's *The Bicycle Thief* and Fellini's *Amarcord,* this is the only venue in Vancouver where you can regularly view the history of cinema. One-year memberships are only five dollars. The Cinémathèque is also accessible on-line at: www.wimsey.com/~jims/cinema.html.

Cineplex Odeon Theatres

Twenty-four-hour film information (604-434-2463)

This first-run theatre chain is the largest in Canada with more than six hundred screens nation-wide. Cineplex Odeon was the innovator of bulk-candy concessions in Vancouver and also serves "real butter" on its popcorn, truly vital innovations for serious filmgoers. Ticket prices are discounted on Tuesdays.

CN IMAX Theatre

201-999 Canada Place (604-682-4629)

Its giant five-storey-high screen and wraparound digital sound make CN Imax one of the world's best places to watch two- and three-dimensional movies. From spectacular footage shot by space-shuttle astronauts, to thrilling nature adventures and larger-than-life concert films, the IMAX experience is one you won't soon forget. Phone ahead for scheduling and special events.

The Disney Store

Eaton Centre, Burnaby (604-668-8125)

Park Royal Mall, West Vancouver (604-981-3025)

The Disney Store has something for the manic Disney buffs among us. Classic movies on video and memorable cartoon characters in every form imaginable are here for the purchasing. A great place for kids to take their parents.

The Edison Electric

916 Commercial Drive (604-255-4162)

It may look like an unassuming hole-in-the-wall, but the Edison Electric is actually a rare venue for independent filmmakers to exhibit their wares. On weekend evenings an eclectic mix of 1950s industrial films, experimental student projects, and the latest from the city's underground can be seen. Call ahead, or drop by for a schedule. Admission is usually five dollars.

Famous Players Theatres

Twenty-four-hour film information (604-681-4255)

The oldest theatre chain in Canada, Famous Players has more than 450 screens across the country and was the first to introduce interactive ticket kiosks. Ticket prices are discounted on Tuesdays.

The Fifth Avenue Cinemas

5th Avenue and Burrard Street (604-734-7469)

Vancouver's premiere art house theatre is also its newest. Opened in the summer of 1996, the Fifth Avenue Cinemas offer five full-sized screens playing first-run Canadian and independent features, Dolby digital stereo, and, of course, a cappuccino bar.

Golden Age Collectables

830 Granville Street (604-683-2819)

Golden Age has been around for more than twenty years and is still the best place to find the latest in cinema and television collectables. The store carries an extensive line of *The X-Files* merchandise, as well as genuine movie onesheets, press kits, screenplays, and much more.

Omnimax Theatre

Science World, 1455 Quebec Street (recorded information: 604-268-6363)

You may want to skip lunch before visiting the Omnimax Theatre at Science World. Watching a film about earthquakes or space travel on the large domed screen can be as exhilarating as a roller coaster ride, but for a few it can also be a bit disorienting.

Orpheum Theatre Showbiz Museum

Smithe Street at Seymour (604-665-3050)

Much of Vancouver's show-biz history is housed within the walls of the Orpheum Theatre. Exhibits of vintage marquee posters, lobby-card photos, autographed stills, and other memorabilia dating back to 1927 are available for viewing as part of a regularly guided tour. Additional information about the heritage building and B.C.'s Entertainment Hall of Fame is available on-line at: www.city.vancouver.bc.ca/theatres/index.html.

Planet Hollywood

750 Burrard Street (opening early 1997)

Billed as "the world's only dining experience inspired by the worlds of film and television," Planet Hollywood was launched in New York in October 1991. It has since spawned dozens of locations around the globe, each housing an extensive collection of movie memorabilia and celebrity palm prints. The ultimate dining experience for insatiable movie buffs. Oh, and the food is California-style cuisine.

Vancouver International Film Festival

410-1008 Homer Street (604-685-0260)

Every year, from late September to mid October, the Vancouver International Film Festival shines the spotlight on world cinema. Close to three hundred movies from around the globe are shown, many for the very first and only time. Films such as *Henry: Portrait of a Serial Killer* and Clint Eastwood's *Bird* have had their Canadian premieres here, and the festival's Asian film series is one of the largest of its kind. To avoid disappointment, book two weeks off work and arrive early. The Vancouver International Film Festival is available on-line at: http://viff.org/viff/.

Vancouver Starwalk

800–900 blocks, Granville Street

If you look closely at the sidewalk along theatre row you'll find more than sixty small circle-encompassed stars inscribed with the names of famous Canadians. The Vancouver Starwalk was inaugurated on July 24, 1994 and, like Hollywood's Walk of Fame, honours those who have made outstanding contributions to the entertainment industries of British Columbia and Canada. Some of the performers include Jeff

Hyslop, Chief Dan George, Dal Richards, Dorothy Davies, Bruno Gerussi, Jack Cullen, Brent Carver, and Jim Byrnes.

Video In

1965 Main Street (604-872-8337)

This access and resource centre for independent video producers and the public offers many how-to workshops as well as exhibitions and a two-thousand-title Canadian and international video library. It is a super hands-on video centre. Its on-line site is located at: www.portal.ca:80/~video/.

Videomatica

1855 West 4th Avenue (604-734-0411)

Videomatica is the city's premiere video rental outlet for discriminating cinephiles. Some of the most unusual titles on laser disc and VHS tape find their way on to Videomatica's shelves, and the staff is arguably the most knowledgeable in town. Visit Videomatica's Sales Outlet, two doors down, for special deals.

On-line Services

Academy of Canadian Cinema and Television

www.everyware.com/academy/

A database for the Genie and Gemini Awards, Canada's version of the Oscars and Emmys.

British Columbia Motion Picture Association

www.bcmpa.bc.ca/

A non-profit umbrella organization with listings of B.C. productions and links of local interest.

Canada Newswire

www.newswire.ca/releases/

Canada's most frequently updated entertainment news releases.

Cinema Canada Online Directory

www.io.org/cincan

A national electronic directory for the Canadian film and TV industry with links to other movie-related sites.

Hollywood North On Line
www.meier.com/meier/meier.html
A Vancouver film industry web page with links to box-office reports, production company listings, classifieds, local film news, and more.

Mandy's Film and Television Production Diary
www.mandy.com/canbc.html
Listings of Vancouver's behind-the-scenes production personnel, production companies, and facilities.

Moving Images
www.movingimages.bc.ca
B.C. distributor's listing of independent filmmakers' catalogue titles.

Reel West
www.reelwest.com
The most comprehensive and complete resource guide for filmmakers working in Western Canada.

Role Call
www.rolecall.com
Behind-the-scenes interviews, profiles, and production listings for Vancouver's film and theatre industries, with links to other movie web sites.

THA Media
www.thamedia.com
B.C.-based film distributor listings of Canadian and international catalogue titles.

Vancouver Film School
www.multimedia.edu
On-line information about one of the most successful film schools.

Vancouver Magazine
www.vanmag.com/Village/Just_In/Buzz.html
Up-to-the-minute local entertainment news and sports scores.

Vancouver On Line
www.coopnet.org/online/Entertainment
More movie and entertainment-related listings for the Vancouver area.

MADE IN BRITISH COLUMBIA

Filmmakers have been capturing British Columbia on celluloid ever since cinema began in the late 1800s. American inventor and producer Thomas Edison arrived to shoot promotional films in the early 1900s, while other filmmakers, impressed with B.C.'s natural beauty, followed in the 1920s.

During the 1930s, Hollywood companies flocked to Victoria to make "quota quickie" films. Movies that qualified as British productions could be easily sold to the protectionist U.K. market for a quick buck. Rita Hayworth got her start starring in "quickies" made by Columbia Pictures, but after the quota system was revised in 1938 (excluding those films made in the dominions) they pulled out of B.C. and the feature film industry seemed to dry up. Though there were a

Spectators look on as a Vancouver street is transformed into San Francisco.

handful of propaganda-inspired movies produced during the Second World War, the 1950s saw B.C.'s feature film market fall on hard times.

The 1960s and 1970s heralded more realism in the movies. Directors such as Robert Altman and Mike Nichols took their productions on the road and filmed entire features on location in and around Vancouver. Altman's *That Cold Day in the Park* was one of the first major films to cast the city as itself.

Exchange rates on the Canadian dollar enticed big American studios to follow in the 1980s. Such hits as *The Accused, Year of the Dragon,* and *The NeverEnding Story* solidified Vancouver's reputation as a first-class production centre, while indigenous films such as *My American Cousin* helped put B.C. on the international filmmaking map.

Though some films shot in the city (especially the many tightly budgeted B-movies) are still the result of a cheap Canadian dollar, the 1990s have seen Vancouver become a major player in the film and television industries, and the third largest production centre in North America.

While it is impossible to chronicle all the films that have been made in B.C., this filmography is one of the most comprehensive ever compiled. The titles listed are for feature films (documentaries, TV movies, and shorts are not included) shot in whole or in part in British Columbia. Unless mentioned otherwise, most films were shot in and around the Greater Vancouver area. Movies have been chronologically and alphabetically arranged under the year they were actually made, while the year listed after a film's genre indicates when it was released (films with no release dates have yet to be released).

1910s

The Cowpuncher's Glove (Drama) 1910
Director: J. Searle Dawley
Cast: Unknown
A pair of cowboys fall for the same girl and resolve matters atop the Capilano Suspension Bridge. Filmed by the Edison Mfg. Company during a tour across Canada to make promotional films for the CPR.

In the Land of the War Canoes (Drama) 1914
Director: Edward S. Curtis
Cast: Unknown
In hopes of gaining power from spirit forces, a young Native man sets out on a vision quest. Director Curtis cast Kwakiutl Natives in the leading roles and filmed on Vancouver Island.

The Ship's Husband (Comedy) 1910
Director: Henry Cronjager
Cast: Unknown
This madcap romp about two couples who believe their spouses are fooling around with each other was made by the Edison Mfg. Company.

The Stolen Claim (Drama) 1910
Director: J. Searle Dawley
Cast: Unknown
The B.C. Rockies are the backdrop for this explosive, and exploding, mining story. Also made by the Edison Mfg. Company.

1920s

The Alaskan (Action/Drama) 1924
Director: Herbert Brenon
Cast: Thomas Meighan, Estelle Taylor, Anna May Wong
While on a sea voyage to the Great White North, an Alaskan landowner meets the woman of his dreams.

The Conflict (Drama) 1921
Director: Stuart Paton
Cast: Priscilla Dean, Edward Connelly, Hector Sarno
A society girl goes to live in the woods with her evil uncle and his wicked housekeeper. Filmed near Cranbrook.

The Eternal Struggle (Drama) 1923
Director: Reginald Barker
Cast: Renee Adoree, Earle Williams, Barbara La Marr
Believing she's responsible for the death of her would-be seducer, a young woman flees to North Vancouver.

The Flaming Forest (Adventure) 1926
Director: Reginald Barker
Cast: Antonio Moreno, Gardner James, William Austin
True-life account of the Riel uprising and the formation of the Royal North West Mounted Police. Filmed near Fort Steele.

Hearts Aflame (Drama) 1922
Director: Reginald Barker
Cast: Frank Keenan, Craig Ward, Stanton Heck
A retired lumberman sends his son to Michigan to clear a logjam, where he promptly falls in love with a woman who refuses to sell her land. Filmed in the East Kootenays.

Policing the Plains (Drama) 1927
Director: A. D. Kean
Cast: Dorothy Fowler, Jack Boyd, Bill Feron
A history of, and tribute to, the Royal Canadian Mounted Police.

Unseeing Eyes (Adventure) 1923
Director: E. H. Griffith
Cast: Lionel Barrymore, Seena Owen, Walter Miller
The sister of a silver mine owner hires a renegade pilot to fly her to her brother's rescue. Filmed near Invermere.

The Wilderness Patrol (Western) 1928
Director: J. P. McGowan
Cast: Bill Cody
This generic western was filmed in North Vancouver and starred Canadian-born Bill Cody, who went on to become one of Hollywood's leading western heroes.

The Winds of Chance (Adventure/Drama) 1925
Director: Frank Lloyd
Cast: Ben Lyons, Anna Q. Nillson, Viola Danna, Victor McLallen
A love triangle set against the turn-of-the-century gold rush. Filmed partially in Dawson City.

1930s

Across the Border (Adventure) 1937
Director: Leon Barsha
Cast: Rita Hayworth, Charles Quigley, George McKay
A customs officer gets mixed up with a gang of fur thieves and a damsel in distress. Filmed in Victoria.

Convicted (Thriller) 1937
Director: Leon Barsha
Cast: Rita Hayworth, Charles Quigley
After a woman is strangled, a dour detective is entrusted to solve the case. Filmed in Victoria.

The Crimson Paradise (Drama) 1933
Director: Robert Hill
Cast: Nick Stuart, Lucille Brown, Kathleen Humphreys
A young man on the skids takes off for B.C. to earn a living as a lumberjack. Victoria locations included Craigdarroch Castle and Beacon Hill Park. It was billed as "Canada's first all-talking motion picture."

Death Goes North (Mystery) 1937
Director: Frank McDonald
Cast: Edgar Edwards, Dorothy Bradshaw, Rin Tin Tin, Jr.
A pair of Mounties find love (presumably not with each other) while investigating a murder. Filmed on Vancouver Island.

Lucky Corrigan (Adventure) 1936
Director: Lewis Collins
Cast: William Gargan, Molly Lamont
Two feuding lumber camps try to outrival each other. Also known as *Fury and the Woman.* Filmed in Victoria.

Lucky Fugitives (Suspense) 1935
Director: Nick Grinde
Cast: Maxine Doyle, David Manners
A famous writer gets into trouble when his "evil twin" escapes from prison. Filmed on Vancouver Island.

Manhattan Shakedown (Mystery) 1937
Director: Leon Barsha
Cast: Rosiland Keith, John Gallaudet, George McKay
This murder mystery, filmed in Victoria, featured a newspaper reporter who suspects a psychiatrist of blackmailing his patients.

Murder Is News (Mystery) 1937
Director: Leon Barsha
Cast: Iris Meredith, John Gallaudet, George McKay
Yes, there were sequels back then! In this Victoria-filmed sequel to *Manhattan Shakedown,* the newspaper reporter now suspects a wealthy industrialist of murdering his wife.

Rose Marie (Musical) 1936
Director: S. S. Van Dyke
Cast: Jeanette MacDonald, Nelson Eddy, James Stewart, Dávid Niven
An opera star sings in a tavern to earn money for her escaped-con brother. Outdoor locations were shot around Vancouver's North Shore and taken back to Hollywood where transparencies were used as backgrounds. Also known as *Indian Love Call,* this was one of Jimmy Stewart's first films.

The Secrets of Chinatown (Mystery) 1934
Director: Fred Newmeyer
Cast: Nick Stuart, Lucille Brown, James Flavin
Vancouver and Victoria stand in for London, England, where a crazed cult of Asian killers is on the loose! Also known as *The Black Robe.*

Secret Patrol (Drama) 1936
Director: David Selman
Cast: Charles Starrett, Fennis Barton
A pair of Mounties, in love with the same girl, investigate a series of highly suspicious accidents.

Silent Barriers (Adventure) 1935
Director: Milton Rosmer
Cast: Richard Arlen, Lilli Palmer
The adventures of roughneck men working on the Canadian railroad. Also known as *The Great Barrier.*

Stampede (Drama) 1936
Director: Ford Beebe
Cast: Charles Starrett, Fennis Barton, J. P. McGowan
A pair of horse traders become entangled in a web of deceit and betrayal. Filmed in Victoria.

Tugboat Princess (Drama) 1936
Director: David Selman
Cast: Walter Kelly, Edith Fellows
Rival captains reconcile a twenty-year feud on the high seas. Filmed in Victoria.

Vengeance (Drama) 1937
Director: Del Lord
Cast: Lyle Talbot, Wendy Barrie
After failing to stop a robbery, a shamed police officer resigns from the force and infiltrates the underworld in an attempt to redeem himself. Filmed in Victoria.

Woman Against the World (Drama) 1937
Director: David Selman
Cast: Ralph Forbes, Grant McDonald, Colette Lyons
A melodramatic tale of a single mom's struggle to survive after being convicted of murder. Filmed in Victoria.

1940s

Canadian Pacific (Drama) 1949
Director: Edwin L. Martin
Cast: Randolph Scott, Jane Wyatt, J. Carroll Naish
An American surveyor helps build the CPR Railway while fighting off attacks from mutinous workers. Filmed in the Rockies and the Fraser Valley.

Commandos Strike at Dawn (Action) 1942
Director: John Farrow
Cast: Paul Muni, Lillian Gish, Cedric Hardwicke, Anna Lee
A resistance fighter battles evil Nazis after they invade Norway.

Corvette K-225 (Adventure) 1943
Director: Richard Rosson
Cast: Randolph Scott, James Brown, Ella Raines, Noah Beery, Jr.
The story of British and Canadian warship escorts, and the men who served aboard them. A Howard Hawks production.

First Comes Courage (Drama) 1943
Director: Dorothy Arzner
Cast: Merle Oberon, Brian Aherne, Carl Esmond, Fritz Leiber
The true-life tale of anti-Nazi resistance fighters in a small Norwegian coastal town. The battle scenes were filmed in Nanaimo and Courtenay.

The 49th Parallel (Suspense/Drama) 1941
Director: Michael Powell
Cast: Laurence Olivier, Leslie Howard, Raymond Massey, Anton Walbrook
A German submarine sinks and its crew escapes to Canada in this Second World War drama that won an Oscar for original screenplay. While scenes shot in the Rockies were integral to the film, footage lensed at the Hotel Vancouver was cut out of the picture before its release. Also known as *The Invaders*.

Johnny Stool Pigeon (Drama) 1949
Director: William Castle
Cast: Shelley Winters, Howard Duff, Dan Duryea
A former Alcatraz inmate helps a U.S. government agent track down drug runners to Vancouver.

Son of Lassie (Family) 1945
Director: Sylvan Simon
Cast: Peter Lawford, Donald Crisp, June Lockhart

After being shot down during the Second World War, Peter Lawford sends his dog, Laddie, for help, but Laddie mistakenly brings back two Nazis! A sequel to *Lassie Come Home*. Filmed on Vancouver Island and in the Rockies.

1950s

Timber Jack (Adventure/Drama) 1950
Director: Joseph Kane
Cast: Sterling Hayden, Vera Ralston, Hoagy Carmichael
A feud between a landowner and a lumberjack leads to death and betrayal. Filmed near Cowichan Lake.

1960s

The Bitter Ash (Drama) 1963
Director: Laurence Kent
Cast: Laurence Kent, Alan Scarfe, Lynne Stewart
An aspiring playwright loses his wife's love to a world of sex and drugs. The University of British Columbia was a handy location for the film's mostly student crew.

Five Easy Pieces (Drama) 1969
Director: Robert Rafelson
Cast: Jack Nicholson, Karen Black, Susan Anspach, Billy Green Bush, Sally Struthers
Classic drama about an oil field worker who returns home to confront his past. Filmed partly in the Gulf Islands.

Great Coups of History (Drama) 1969
Director: Jack Darcus
Cast: Delphine Harvey, Jani Cassi
While a middle-aged woman talks about past sexual conquests, her teenaged daughter deals with her own sexuality.

The Mad Room (Horror) 1968
Director: Bernard Girard
Cast: Stella Stevens, Shelley Winters, Skip Ward, Carol Cole, Beverly Garland, Michael Burns, Barbara Sammeth
Heads roll (literally) as a pair of institutionalized siblings come to stay with their aunt and widowed companion. A remake of the 1941 film *Ladies in Retirement*.

The Plastic Mile (Drama) 1969
Director: Morrie Ruvinsky
Cast: Jace Van Der Veen, Pia Shandel, Cece Grandbois
Featuring Vancouver broadcaster Pia Shandel, this controversial film tells of a director who endures a crisis while shooting an erotic movie. Also known as *Finishing Touch* and *She's a Woman*.

The Sweet and the Bitter (Drama) 1962
Director: James Clavell
Cast: Yoko Tani, Paul Richards, Jane Mallet, Peter Haworth
A Japanese girl moves to Canada, Steveston specifically, with hopes of avenging her father's wartime death.

Sweet Substitute (Drama) 1964
Director: Laurence Kent
Cast: Robert Howay, Angela Gann, Carol Pastinsky
Sexploitational tale of a college lad who wins a scholarship and loses his virginity. Also known as *Caressed*.

That Cold Day in the Park (Drama) 1969
Director: Robert Altman
Cast: Sandy Dennis, Michael Burns, Suzanne Benton, Luana Anders, John Garfield, Jr., Michael Murphy
Repressed sexuality gets the best of an emotionally disturbed woman after she invites a young man in out of the Vancouver rain. One of Altman's first films.

The Trap (Adventure/Drama) 1966
Director: Sydney Hayers
Cast: Oliver Reed, Rita Tushingham, Rex Sevenoaks
A mute orphan girl falls in love with a rough-and-tumble trapper in spite of herself. Shot in the Pemberton Valley.

Waiting for Caroline (Drama) 1967
Director: Ron Kelly
Cast: Sharon Acker, Robert Howay, Alexandra Stewart
A teenaged girl is torn between Vancouver and Montreal, and the lovers she has in each city.

When Tomorrow Dies (Drama) 1965
Director: Laurence Kent
Cast: Patricia Gage, Douglas Campbell, Neil Dainard
A married middle-aged woman returns to school and has an affair with her professor. Vancouver director Laurence Kent won the Vancouver International Film Festival's Centennial Prize for this, his third Vancouver-made feature.

1970

Explosion (Drama) 1970
Director: Jules Bricken
Cast: Don Stroud, Gordon Thompson, Michele Chicoine, Cece Linder
An American draft-dodger and a Vancouver hippie become embroiled in a strange murder. Also known as *The Wrong Mountain* and *Blast*.

Kemek (Thriller) 1971
Director: Jack McCallum
Cast: Mary Woronov, Chuck Mitchell, Cal Haines
This strange detective thriller was originally filmed in Italy. The picture was purchased by McCallum, then cut by forty minutes and the missing pieces replaced with Vancouver-lensed footage.

The Life and Times of Chester Angus Ramsgood (Comedy) 1970
Director: Don Wilson
Cast: Robert Matson, Mary Beth McGuffin, Michael Storgeoff
A clumsy young man schemes to win the affections of his dream girl, and lose his virginity.

McCabe and Mrs. Miller (Western) 1970
Director: Robert Altman
Cast: Warren Beatty, Julie Christie, Rene Auberjonois, Shelley Duvall, Terry David Mulligan
A small town drifter and a country madam team up to build a luxury brothel (near Capilano Canyon) in this classic turn-of-the-century comedy-drama. Notable also for supporting role by local broadcast personality Terry David Mulligan.

A Name for Evil (Horror) 1970
Director: Barney Girard
Cast: Robert Culp, Samantha Eggar
A couple takes up residence in a spooky old house where a ghost seduces the wife. Also known as *The Grove* and *The Face of Evil*.

1971

Another Smith for Paradise (Comedy) 1971
Director: Thomas Shandel
Cast: Henry Ramer, Frances Hyland, Pia Shandel
A libertine wife and federal tax investigators complicate the plans of a Ukrainian-Canadian financier. Local broadcaster Pia Shandel, who was the wife of director Thomas Shandel, makes an appearance as Ramer's college-aged daughter.

Carnal Knowledge (Drama) 1971
Director: Mike Nichols
Cast: Jack Nicholson, Candice Bergen, Art Garfunkel, Ann-Margret
Vancouver stands in for New York and more, as North America's Me-Decade sexual dilemmas are given the once-over by two college buddies who chronicle their sex lives over three decades.

The Groundstar Conspiracy (Science Fiction) 1972
Director: Lamont Johnson
Cast: George Peppard, Michael Sarrazin, Christine Belford, Cliff Potts
In this sci-fi-spy thriller, a secret space station is destroyed and the only man with answers has been stricken with amnesia. Based on the L. P. Davies novel *The Alien*.

Madeleine Is (Drama) 1971
Director: Sylvia Spring
Cast: Nicole Lipman, John Juliani, Wayne Sprecht
A young French-Canadian girl flees to the west coast in hopes of finding herself.

Proxyhawks (Drama) 1971
Director: Jack Darcus
Cast: Jack Darcus, Susan Spencer, Ed Hutchings, Leslie Rachuk, Barry Jones
Vancouver filmmaker Jack Darcus's strange socio-political allegory about a man and a woman, a farm and their animals.

1972

In Pursuit of (Romantic Comedy) 1973
Director: Richard Walton
Cast: Rex Owen, Cecilia Smith
Made on a shoestring budget by an American businessman who fancied himself a director, this comedic love story with an upbeat message was shot around Jericho Park.

Master of Images (Cult) 1972
Director: Byron Black
Cast: Byron Black, Lulu Uhul, Neils Ashby, Bill Rykers, Tony White
Amusing film about a karma-troubled young woman and her similarly plagued friends.

1973

Harry in Your Pocket (Drama) 1973
Director: Art Jones
Cast: James Coburn, Michael Sarrazin, Trish Van Devere, Walter Pidgeon
Everything you've always wanted to know about pickpockets, and quite a bit more. Filmed in Victoria.

One Minute Before Death (Horror) 1973
Director: Rogelio Gonzales
Cast: Wanda Hendrix, Giselle McKenzie, Barry Coe
Filmed in an upscale Shaughnessy mansion, this bizarre murder mystery flick is strictly for fans of the occult.

The Oval Portrait (Horror) 1973
Director: Rogelio Gonzales
Cast: Wanda Hendrix, Giselle McKenzie, Barry Coe
Another run-of-the-mill haunted house yarn brought to you by the people who made *One Minute Before Death*. Inspired by an Edgar Allan Poe story.

The Rainbow Gang (Comedy/Drama) 1973
Director: Gerald Patterson
Cast: Donald Pleasance, Don Calfa, Kate Reid
Three unlikely prospectors search for fame and fortune in the wilds of British Columbia's mile-high mountains. Also known as *The Rainbow Boys*.

Sexcula (Cult) 1973
Director: John Holbrook
Cast: All pseudonyms
A sex-crazed female scientist builds a monster that's impotent, then has her cousin, Sexcula, try to arouse it.

Sunshine (Drama) 1973
Director: Joseph Sargent
Cast: Christina Raines, Cliff DeYoung, Brenda Vaccaro
Made for TV but released theatrically in Vancouver and Europe, this melodrama tells of a young mother who decides to live with her incurable cancer rather than have her leg amputated.

1974

Christina (Suspense) 1974
Director: Paul Krasny
Cast: Barbara Parkins, Peter Haskell
A mysterious and beautiful woman pays a forlorn fella to marry her, then disappears as he begins to fall in love.

Dogpound Shuffle (Musical/Comedy) 1974
Director: Jeffrey Bloom
Cast: Ron Moody, David Soul
This British-made farce finds two has-been entertainers trying to raise money to get their dog out of the pound.

The Holy Assassin (Science Fiction) 1974
Director: Byron Black
Cast: Byron Black, Lulu McMovie, Joan McIntyre, Fred Flores
A metaphysical criminal from another dimension tries to fit in with Vancouver's hippie culture. A precursor to the cult film *The Man Who Fell to Earth*, sort of.

The Inbreaker (Drama) 1974
Director: George McGowan
Cast: Christopher George, Johnny Crawford
A young man goes to work in the fishing industry and finds that life just isn't what he'd hoped it would be.

The Naked Man (Drama) 1974
Director: Rogelio Gonzales
Cast: Jose Alonzo, Irma Lazano
From the makers of *One Minute Before Death* and *The Oval Portrait* comes another Mexican B-grade scare-'em-up romp.

Shanks (Horror) 1974
Director: William Castle
Cast: Marcel Marceau, Tsilla Chelton
A bizarre tale of a mute puppeteer who brings dead bodies back to life. This was William Castle's last film as a director.

The Wolfpen Principle (Drama) 1974
Director: Jack Darcus
Cast: Vladimir Valenta, Doris Chilcott, Laurence Brown, Alicia Ammon
A theatre (the Varsity on West 10th Avenue) manager helps a First Nations boy set wolves free from captivity.

1975

The Bears and I (Family) 1975
Director: Bernard McEveety
Cast: Patrick Wayne, Chief Dan George, Andrew Duggan
While raising three bear cubs, a young Vietnam vet helps Native people regain their land.

Food of the Gods (Science Fiction) 1976
Director: Bert Gordon
Cast: Marjoe Gortner, Pamela Franklin, Ida Lupino
Giant chickens and rats crave human flesh on a deserted island (and at the PNE's old Empire Stadium). This film, based on the H. G. Wells novel, actually spawned a sequel!

Jaws of Death (Suspense) 1975
Director: Richard Martin
Cast: Arthur Franz, James Hunter
No description available.

Journey into Fear (Suspense) 1975
Director: Daniel Mann
Cast: Sam Waterston, Yvette Mimieux, Vincent Price, Donald Pleasance, Joseph Wiseman, Shelley Winters, Zero Mostel
While on a ship bound for Italy, a research geologist finds that someone is trying to kill him. A remake of Orson Welles's 1942 adaptation of Eric Ambler's novel.

Russian Roulette (Thriller) 1975
Director: Lou Lombardo
Cast: George Segal, Christina Raines, Bo Brundin, Denholm Elliott, Louise Fletcher
A plot to assassinate a visiting Soviet premier is uncovered by an RCMP corporal. Vancouver stars as itself.

Sally Fieldgood and Company (Drama) 1976
Director: Boon Collins
Cast: Hagen Beggs, Valerie Ambrose
A gambler takes up with his ex-lover and gets involved in a wild money-making scheme.

The Supreme Kid (Adventure) 1975
Director: Peter Bryant
Cast: Frank Moore, Helen Shaver, Don Granberry, Terry David Mulligan
The ragtag adventures of a couple of modern-day hobos and the people whose lives they cross. This was not only the first feature film completed by an alumnus of Simon Fraser University's Film Workshop, but also one of Helen Shaver's first on-screen appearances.

1976

Death Hunt (Drama) 1976
Director: Timothy Galfas
Cast: Mike Connors, Jennifer Swope
The compelling tale of a man bent on revenge after his wife is attacked on a camping trip. Also known as *Revenge for a Rape*. Made locally for television but released theatrically overseas.

Shadow of the Hawk (Action) 1976
Director: Daryl Duke
Cast: Jan-Michael Vincent, Chief Dan George, Marilyn Hassett, Pia Shandel
Supernatural ghosts chase a young man of Native descent all over the Interior of British Columbia.

1977

Ants (Horror) 1977
Director: Robert Scheerer
Cast: Lynda Day George, Myrna Loy, Suzanne Somers, Robert Foxworth
Insecticide-infected ants feed on unsuspecting guests at a motel. Also known as *Panic at Lakewood Manor* and *It Happened at Lakewood Manor*. Made locally for television but released theatrically overseas.

Le Menace (Suspense) 1977
Director: Alain Corneau
Cast: Yves Montand, Carol Laure
A rich and beautiful woman is murdered after she discovers her lover is having an affair. Also known as *The Threat.*

The Other Side of the Mountain-Part 2 (Romance) 1977
Director: Larry Peerce
Cast: Marilyn Hassett, Timothy Bottoms
The sequel to the 1975 tearjerker recounting the true story of paralysed Olympic downhill skier Jill Kinmont.

Skip Tracer (Drama) 1977
Director: Zale Dalen
Cast: David Peterson, John Lazarus
A debt collector teaches a new employee the tricks of the trade and gets more than he bargained for.

1978

Kavik the Wolf Dog (Adventure) 1978
Director: Peter Carter
Cast: Ronny Cox, John Ireland, John Candy
A champion sled dog loses his nerve after a near fatal airplane crash, but must confront his fears as he journeys from Alaska, through the wilds of British Columbia, and home to Seattle.

The Keeper (Horror) 1984
Director: Tom Drake
Cast: Christopher Lee, Sally Gray, Pia Shandel
An evil asylum operator preys on the wealthy in this cash-for-crazies spoof on the horror genre.

A Man, a Woman and a Bank (Suspense/Comedy) 1979
Director: Noel Black
Cast: Donald Sutherland, Paul Mazursky, Brooke Adams
Two men who plan on engaging in a white-collar bank heist get more than they bargained for when an advertising agency woman falls for one of the would-be thieves. Also called *A Very Big Weekend.*

Prophecy (Horror) 1978
Director: John Frankenheimer
Cast: Talia Shire, Robert Foxworth, Armand Assante, Richard Dysart
This eco-horror tale about a doctor and his wife researching the effects of pollution in a Maine lumber town was filmed partially in North Vancouver.

1979

Bear Island (Suspense) 1980
Director: Don Sharp
Cast: Vanessa Redgrave, Donald Sutherland, Richard Widmark
A British-Canadian adaptation of Alistair MacLean's book in which secret agents disguised as weather researchers search for a Nazi submarine. Great B.C. scenery but an uninspiring film.

The Changeling (Horror) 1980
Director: Peter Medak
Cast: George C. Scott, Trish Van Devere, Barry Morse
Vancouver doubles for Seattle as a recently widowed composer moves into a haunted house. Winner of Canada's Genie Award for best picture.

Klondike Fever (Adventure) 1979
Director: Peter Carter
Cast: Rod Steiger, Angie Dickinson, Lorne Greene
Jack London travels to the Klondike in search of fame and fortune. Also known as *Jack London's Klondike Fever*. Featuring B.C.'s Barkerville.

Out of the Blue (Drama) 1981
Director: Dennis Hopper
Cast: Linda Manz, Dennis Hopper, Raymond Burr
A gritty examination of a troubled teen's relationship with her ex-con father. New Westminster's Raymond Burr co-stars.

Seasons in the Sun (Drama) 1979
Director: Ain Sooder
Cast: Terry Jacks, Kathryn Witt
Taking its title from Terry Jacks's 1973 hit song, *Seasons in the Sun* tells of a rock star, played by Jacks, who discovers he has a debilitating disease and decides to move to British Columbia. Here he becomes involved with a Russian secret agent.

Strange Companions (Drama) 1979
Director: Frank Zuniga
Cast: Doug McClure, Michael Sharrett
No description available.

Up River (Drama) 1979
Director: Carl Kitt
Cast: Jeff Corey, Morgan Stevens
After his wife is killed and his land taken away, a pioneer swears vengeance against the man responsible.

1980

Big Meat Eater (Musical/Comedy) 1980
Director: Chris Windsor
Cast: Big Miller, George Dawson
Cult film about a bunch of aliens who use radioactive butcher's discards to fuel their spaceship. Also known as *The Butcher of Burquitlam.*

By Design (Drama) 1981
Director: Claude Jutra
Cast: Patty Duke Astin, Sarah Botsford, Saul Rubinek
A lesbian couple decide they want to have a baby and embark on a search for a willing stud.

Crossover (Drama) 1982
Director: John Guillerman
Cast: James Coburn, Kate Nelligan
A male nurse's personal life is neglected when he works the late shift at a psychiatric ward. Also known as *Mr. Patman*.

The Grey Fox (Western) 1982
Director: Phillip Borsos
Cast: Richard Farnsworth, Jackie Burroughs
After serving a thirty-year jail sentence, Canadian stagecoach robber Billy Miner is released into the twentieth century. Much of the film was shot around Merritt and Cranbrook and is based on a true story. Winner of the Genie Award for best picture, best supporting actress, and best director.

Harry Tracy (Western) 1982
Director: William A. Graham
Cast: Bruce Dern, Helen Shaver
A gentleman outlaw can't seem to stay out of trouble until he meets the woman of his dreams. Also known as *Harry Tracy—Desperado*. Filmed in Victoria.

The High Country (Drama) 1980
Director: Harvey Hart
Cast: Timothy Bottoms, Linda Purl
A maladjusted woman and an escaped drug dealer find solace together at a mountain retreat in British Columbia's Rockies.

Ladies and Gentlemen, The Fabulous Stains (Cult) 1981
Director: Lou Adler
Cast: Diane Lane, Peter Donat, Laura Dern, Christine Lahti
A rebellious teenaged girl decides to become a punk rocker. Members of The Clash and The Sex Pistols appear as a British punk band, and Vancouver high school kids can be seen dancing and screaming. One of Diane Lane's first film appearances.

Never Cry Wolf (Drama) 1983
Director: Carroll Ballard
Cast: Charles Martin Smith, Brian Dennehy
A lone researcher lives among the wolves of the Arctic. Based on the book by Farley Mowatt and filmed near Stewart.

Quest for Fire (Drama) 1981
Director: Jean-Jacques Annaud
Cast: Everett McGill, Rae Dawn Chong, Ron Perlman, Nameer El-Kadi
Ice Age men look for fire to save their tribes in this dawn-of-mankind

opus that was partially filmed in B.C.'s Interior.

Reckless (Romance/Drama) 1982
Director: Dgordge Milicevic
Cast: Meg Foster, Robin Mossley, Amy Gibson
An older woman and a younger man get acquainted against the backdrop of motocross racing.

Touch the Wind (Drama) 1980
Director: Christopher Chapman
Cast: Robert Logan, Twyla-Dawn Vokins, Doug Lennox
A rebellious young girl learns to live and love with the help of her bush-pilot father. Also known as *Kelly.*

Virus (Science Fiction) 1980
Director: Kinji Fukasaku
Cast: George Kennedy, Chuck Connors, Glenn Ford
With the exception of a few lucky people who are on a polar expedition, war and plague wipe out the earth's population.

1981

Dead Wrong (Comedy) 1981
Director: Len Kowalewich
Cast: Britt Ekland, Winston Rekert, Jackson Davies
A female undercover agent is sent to track a group of bumbling smugglers. BCTV news anchor Tony Parsons produced this comedy, which is also known as *The Columbian Connection.*

First Blood (Action) 1982
Director: Ted Kotcheff
Cast: Sylvester Stallone, Richard Crenna, Brian Dennehy
A Vietnam vet goes ballistic after being detained by a small town sheriff. This film, which spawned the series of *Rambo* sequels, was filmed partially in Hope.

Mother Lode (Adventure) 1982
Director: Charlton Heston
Cast: Charlton Heston, Nick Mancuso, Kim Basinger
Played out against the terrain of British Columbia, twin brothers (played by Heston) battle each other in an all-consuming hunt for gold. Heston's son Fraser wrote and produced the film.

The Thing (Science Fiction) 1982
Director: John Carpenter
Cast: Kurt Russell, Wilford Brimley, Richard Dysart
A strange alien life form, lodged in ice for millions of years, comes to life after a research team digs it up in the Antarctic. A remake of the 1951 classic of the same name. Filmed near Stewart.

Ups and Downs (Drama) 1983
Director: Paul Almond
Cast: Colin Skinner, Andrew Sabiston, Gavin Brannan
A group of teenagers learns to live and love within the confines of their well-to-do private school.

1982

The Deserters (Comedy) 1982
Director: Jack Darcus
Cast: Alan Scarfe, Jon Bryden
A dark comedy about an American army sergeant who heads to Canada to track down a Vietnam draft-dodger.

Eureka (Adventure) 1983
Director: Nicolas Roeg
Cast: Gene Hackman, Theresa Russell, Joe Pesci, Rutger Hauer, Mickey Rourke
The bizarre tale of a gold miner who learns the error of wishing for too much after he strikes it rich. Based on the book by Paul Mayersberg.

The Golden Seal (Drama) 1982
Director: Frank Zuniga
Cast: Steve Railsback, Penelope Milford, Torquil Campbell
A small boy befriends a rare golden seal and her pups.

Iceman (Science Fiction/Drama) 1984
Director: Fred Schepisi
Cast: Timothy Hutton, Lindsay Crouse, John Lone, Danny Glover
After a frozen Cro-Magnon man is discovered and thawed out, he has trouble coping with the twentieth century. Filmed near Stewart.

Packin' It In (Comedy) 1982
Director: Jud Taylor
Cast: Richard Benjamin, Paula Prentiss, Molly Ringwald
Beautiful British Columbia doubles as the Oregon woods in a comedy about a Los Angeles family who encounter a band of survivalists after relocating to live a quieter life.

The Ruffian (Adventure) 1982
Director: Jose Giovanni
Cast: Lino Venturo, Claudia Cardinale
A mine worker gets mixed up with a band of thieves in search of precious metals.

Spacehunter: Adventures in the Forbidden Zone (Science Fiction) 1983
Director: Lamont Johnson
Cast: Peter Strauss, Molly Ringwald, Ernie Hudson, Michael Ironside
Good-guy bounty hunter takes on bad-guy cyborg while rescuing three damsels in distress. Shot in 3-D.

Star 80 (Drama) 1983
Director: Bob Fosse
Cast: Mariel Hemingway, Eric Roberts, Cliff Robertson
The tragic true-life story of Vancouver's Dorothy Stratten, her climb to stardom and brutal death. Director Bob Fosse chose to film scenes locally for authenticity. This was his last picture.

Strange Brew (Comedy) 1983
Director: Dave Thomas, Rick Moranis
Cast: Dave Thomas, Rick Moranis, Max von Sydow
SCTV's Bob and Doug MacKenzie thwart an evil brewmeister's plans for world domination.

Young Warriors (Comedy/Drama) 1983
Director: Lawrence Foldes
Cast: Ernest Borgnine, Lynda Day George, Richard Roundtree, Dick Shawn
Strange mix of sex, comedy, and violence in a sermonizing story about frat boys turned vigilante.

1983

The Eve of Invasion (Cult) 1984
Director: Neil Campbell
Cast: Mike Robbins, David Armstrong
The abstract adventures of a displaced alien in search of a sense of belonging.

Finders Keepers (Comedy) 1983
Director: Richard Lester
Cast: Lou Gossett, Jr., Michael O'Keefe, Beverly D'Angelo, Jim Carrey
Slapstick romp about a train full of crazy characters in search of $5 million.

The Glitter Dome (Action) 1984
Director: Stuart Margolin
Cast: James Garner, Stuart Margolin, John Lithgow, Margot Kidder
Old-fashioned Victoria stands in for Los Angeles as a pair of policemen discover the sleazier side of Hollywood while investigating the death of a pornographer. Made for TV but released theatrically overseas.

My Kind of Town (Romance) 1983
Director: Charles Wilkinson
Cast: Peter Smith, John Cooper, Illena Paul
A small-town boy yearns for the bright lights of the big city.

The NeverEnding Story (Fantasy) 1984
Director: Wolfgang Petersen
Cast: Barrett Oliver, Noah Hathaway
A young boy takes refuge in the pages of a magical book and becomes the hero. Two more sequels would follow this popular child's fantasy film.

Reno and the Doc (Drama) 1984
Director: Charles Dennis
Cast: Linda Griffiths, Kenneth Walsh, Henry Ramer
A pair of cranky middle-aged men battle their mid-life crises by taking up downhill ski racing.

The Terry Fox Story (Docu-Drama) 1983
Director: Ralph Thomas
Cast: Robert Duvall, Eric Fryer, Chris Makepeace
The story of Canada's Terry Fox and his one-legged "Marathon of Hope" to raise awareness for cancer research. Winner of the Genie Award for best picture and best actor, Eric Fryer.

1984

Blackout (Mystery) 1985
Director: Douglas Hickox
Cast: Richard Widmark, Keith Carradine, Kathleen Quinlan
An obsessive cop hunts for the culprit in a six-year-old murder.

A Certain Fury (Action) 1985
Director: Stephen Gyllenhaal
Cast: Tatum O'Neal, Irene Cara, Peter Fonda, Nicholas Campbell
Two women must keep ahead of both the cops and drug dealers after being mistaken for a pair of prostitutes who shot up a courthouse.

Clan of the Cave Bear (Fantasy) 1985
Director: Michael Chapman
Cast: Daryl Hannah, Pamela Reed, Thomas Waites
A young cavegirl is taken in by Neanderthals in this ponderous prehistory lesson based on the book by Jean M. Auel. Filmed near Stewart and Victoria.

The Journey of Natty Gann (Adventure) 1986
Director: Jeremy Kagan
Cast: Meredith Salenger, John Cusack, Ray Wise
A depression-era adventure about a young girl riding the rails in hopes of finding her father. Some West End heritage houses doubled as 1930s homesteads.

Low Visibility (Drama) 1984
Director: Patricia Gruben
Cast: Larry Lillo, David Peterson, Penelope Stella
An amnesiac found wandering along a snowy mountain roadside arouses the curiosity of the town locals.

My American Cousin (Comedy) 1986
Director: Sandy Wilson
Cast: Margaret Langrick, John Wildman, Richard Donat
A twelve-year-old girl is enthralled by her cool cousin who has come to visit for the summer. Filmed in Penticton, B.C. Director Sandy Wilson won Genie Awards for best picture and best director. A best actor Genie also went to John Wildman.

Regeneration (Cult) 1987
Director: Russell Stephens
Cast: John Anderson, Marek Cieszewski, Dermot Hennelly
A scientist discovers how to bring the dead back to life.

Runaway (Science Fiction) 1985
Director: Michael Crichton
Cast: Tom Selleck, Cynthia Rhodes, Gene Simmons, Kirstie Alley
Vancouver plays the ultimate city of the future in which killer robots are running amok.

Secrets of a Married Man (Drama) 1984
Director: William A. Graham
Cast: William Shatner, Cybill Shepherd
A married man falls for the neighbourhood prostitute.

Walls (Drama) 1985
Director: Michael Chechik
Cast: Winston Rekert, Andree Pelletier
The human spirit is given a good workout in this angst-ridden prison drama.

Year of the Dragon (Action) 1985
Director: Michael Cimino
Cast: Mickey Rourke, John Lone, Ariane
Vancouver's east side stands in for New York in this Oliver Stone-scripted film about a racist police captain assigned to clean up gangland Chinatown.

1985

Abducted (Action) 1985
Director: Boon Collins
Cast: Roberta Weiss, Lawrence King Phillip, Dan Haggerty
A crazed mountain man goes off his rocker and kidnaps a helpless jogger. This locally lensed film actually produced a sequel!

April Fool's Day (Horror) 1985
Director: Fred Walton
Cast: Jay Baker, Deborah Foreman, Griffin O'Neal
A bunch of college kids spend spring break on a desolate island and are the victims of an interminable series of practical and not-so-practical jokes.

The Boy Who Could Fly (Fantasy/Drama) 1985
Director: Nick Castle
Cast: Colleen Dewhurst, Jay Underwood, Lucy Deakins, Fred Savage
After his parents are killed in a plane crash, a young boy retreats into a fantasy world where he can fly.

Bullies (Horror) 1986
Director: Paul Lynch
Cast: Jonathan Crombie, Janet Laine Green, Olivia D'Abo
A young man and his family move to the Ozarks and encounter trouble from the local hillbillies. Filmed in Cranbrook.

Captive Hearts (Drama) 1986
Director: Duncan Gibbons
Cast: Virginia Madsen, Craig Sheffer
The coming-of-age tale of two young star-crossed lovers and their misadventures.

High Stakes (Comedy) 1986
Director: Laurence Kent
Cast: Dave Foley, Roberta Weiss, Winston Rekert
A young cub reporter with dreams of stardom uncovers wacky criminal goings-on. *Kids in the Hall* star David Foley makes his big-screen debut.

Rocky IV (Drama) 1986
Director: Sylvester Stallone
Cast: Sylvester Stallone, Talia Shire, Dolph Lundgren, Carl Weathers
In this third sequel to the 1976 Oscar-winning film, Rocky avenges the death of a good friend and saves the boxing world from communism. Former B.C. Lions' linebacker Carl Weathers co-stars.

The Stepfather (Thriller) 1986
Director: Joseph Ruben
Cast: Terry O'Quinn, Shelley Hack, Jill Schoelen

A psychotic killer in search of the perfect family poses as the ideal father. Filmed partially in Howe Sound.

Striker's Mountain (Action) 1986
Director: Allen Simmonds
Cast: Bruce Greenwood, Leslie Nielsen, Mimi Kuzyk
Big business tries to corrupt a small-time resort owner. Whistler-Blackcomb and other local mountains provide great backdrops for the film's skiing scenes.

1986

An American Gothic (Horror) 1986
Director: John Hugh
Cast: Rod Steiger, Yvonne DeCarlo, Michael J. Pollard
A creepy family disrupts a vacation on a remote desolate island. Also known as *Hide and Shriek.* Filmed on Bowen Island.

Backfire (Mystery) 1986
Director: Gilbert Cates
Cast: Karen Allen, Keith Carradine, Jeff Fahey
This made-in-Victoria film tells the tale of a mysterious stranger who slowly convinces a wealthy Vietnam vet that he's crazy.

Home Is Where the Hart Is (Comedy) 1986
Director: Rex Bromfield
Cast: Valri Bromfield, Stephen E. Miller, Leslie Nielsen, Martin Mull
A bunch of over-the-hill siblings set out to rescue their kidnapped father in this black comedy for the geriatric set.

Hot Pursuit (Comedy) 1987
Director: Steven Lisberger
Cast: John Cusack, Robert Loggia, Wendy Gazelle
After being left behind on a trip to the tropics, a shy prep school student chases down his girlfriend and her parents.

Housekeeping (Drama) 1986
Director: Bill Forsyth
Cast: Christine Lahti, Andrea Burchill, Sarah Walker
A transient comes to the Pacific Northwest to care for her two orphaned nieces. Based on the book by Marilynne Robinson, and filmed in Nelson, this was Scottish director Bill Forsyth's first North American feature.

Malone (Action) 1986
Director: Harley Cokliss
Cast: Burt Reynolds, Cliff Robertson, Lauren Hutton
An ex-CIA agent sets out to right some wrongs done to the locals of a small Oregon town. Filmed in Princeton and Hedley.

Roxanne (Comedy) 1986
Director: Fred Schepisi
Cast: Steve Martin, Daryl Hannah, Shelley Duvall
Martin stars as a big-nosed, small-town, fire chief in this very funny modern-day retelling of the classic "Cyrano de Bergerac." Filmed in Nelson.

1987

The Accused (Drama) 1987
Director: Jonathan Kaplan
Cast: Jodie Foster, Kelly McGillis, Bernie Coulson, Steve Antin
A compelling drama based on the infamous New Bedford, Massachusetts, gang rape trial. Foster gives an Oscar-winning performance as the young woman who seeks justice for what was done to her.

Distant Thunder (Drama) 1987
Director: Rick Rosenthal
Cast: John Lithgow, Ralph Macchio

A Vietnam vet reunites with his estranged son after spending years as a recluse in the woods of Washington State. Filmed in Squamish.

The Experts (Comedy) 1989
Director: Dave Thomas
Cast: John Travolta, Arye Gross, Charles Martin Smith, Kelly Preston
Two nightclub entrepreneurs are kidnapped by the KGB so they can become spies for the Soviet Union.

Shoot to Kill (Action) 1988
Director: Roger Spottiswoode
Cast: Sidney Poitier, Tom Berenger, Kirstie Alley
A city cop and a mountain guide form an unlikely alliance and track a killer to Vancouver. This film marked Poitier's return to the big screen after a ten-year absence.

Stakeout (Action/Comedy) 1987
Director: John Badham
Cast: Richard Dreyfuss, Emilio Estevez, Madeleine Stowe, Aidan Quinn
While two policemen lay in wait for the return of an escaped convict, one of them gets romantically involved with the con's girlfriend. Vancouver doubles as Seattle.

1988

American Boyfriends (Drama) 1989
Director: Sandy Wilson
Cast: Margaret Langrick, John Wildman
The young girl from *My American Cousin* has grown up, and this time it's her turn to do the visiting. The film begins at Simon Fraser University and winds up south of the border, in California.

The Bear (Adventure) 1989
Director: Jean-Jacques Annaud
Cast: Jack Wallace, Tcheky Karyo, Andre Lacombe
The spectacular B.C. Rockies augment this family picture about the adventures of an orphaned bear cub and his surrogate papa. Annaud received France's Cesar Award for best director.

Beyond the Stars (Science Fiction/Adventure) 1989
Director: David Saperstein
Cast: Martin Sheen, Christian Slater, Olivia D'Abo, F. Murray Abraham, Robert Foxworth, Sharon Stone
A whiz kid discovers a deadly accident that occurred during NASA's Apollo 11 moon landing. Filmed near Deep Cove.

Cold Front (Drama) 1989
Director: Allan Goldstein
Cast: Martin Sheen, Michael Ontkean, Beverly D'Angelo, Kim Coates
A pair of determined police officers hunt down a serial killer through Vancouver's mean streets.

Cousins (Drama) 1989
Director: Joel Schumacher
Cast: Ted Danson, Isabella Rossellini, Sean Young, Lloyd Bridges
Remake of the classic French film *Cousin, Cousine* about two people who fall in love despite their families. Vancouver has seldom looked better than it does in this film.

Empire of Ash 3 (Science Fiction) 1989
Director: Lloyd Simandl
Cast: Scott Anderson, Nancy Pataki, Joe Maffei, Tanya Orton
Road Warrior-like tale of an apocalyptic future where mankind has been ravaged by a fatal virus.

The First Season (Drama) 1989
Director: Ralph Thomas
Cast: Kate Trotter, R. H. Thomson, Christianne Hirt
A widowed housewife is determined

to make a go of her departed husband's debt-ridden fishing trawler.

The Fly 2 (Science Fiction) 1989
Director: Chris Walas
Cast: Eric Stoltz, Daphne Zuniga, Lee Richardson
In this sequel to David Cronenberg's *The Fly*, son of fly is born and ages at a rapid rate, before turning into a giant mutant . . . fly!

Immediate Family (Drama) 1988
Director: Jonathan Kaplan
Cast: Glenn Close, James Wood, Mary Stuart Masterson
A wealthy couple who can't have their own children adopt the baby of a down-on-her-luck teenager. Vancouver doubles for Seattle.

Kingsgate (Drama) 1989
Director: Jack Darcus
Cast: Christopher Plummer, Roberta Maxwell, Duncan Fraser
The relationship between a university professor and his student-cum-lover is put to the test when they visit a famous writer and his wife.

Lighthouse (Thriller) 1989
Director: Paul Tucker
Cast: Stephen E. Miller, Debra Wakeham
When a young couple retreat to a lighthouse to sort out their lives, a poltergeist intervenes with their plans. Filmed in Victoria.

Look Who's Talking (Comedy) 1989
Director: Amy Heckerling
Cast: John Travolta, Kirstie Alley
Bruce Willis provides the voice for Mikey, a wisecracking newborn baby who watches and comments on the lives of his mother and babysitter. Vancouver doubles as Manhattan.

Love and Murder (Suspense) 1988
Director: Steven Stern
Cast: Kathleen Lasky, Wayne Robson, Todd Waring
A *Rear Window*-ish tale of a photographer suspected of murder.

Matinee (Horror) 1989
Director: Richard Martin
Cast: Jeff Schultz, Gillian Barber, William B. Davis
A series of murders at a small-town horror-movie film festival has the local sheriff baffled. The interior of the Vogue theatre gets a good workout in this locally produced B-flick.

Quarantine (Science Fiction) 1989
Director: Charles Wilkinson
Cast: Beatrice Boepple, Garwin Sanford, Jerry Wasserman
In an apocalyptic future, quarantine camps for the carriers of a fatal virus are the norm. But for a rebel inventor who must follow his heart, liberation or extermination is the only solution.

Watchers (Science Fiction) 1988
Director: Jon Hess
Cast: Corey Haim, Barbara Williams, Michael Ironside
After finding a super-intelligent pooch, a teenaged boy becomes the target of a scientifically created monster. Watch for an early on-screen appearance by Jason Priestly.

We're No Angels (Comedy) 1989
Director: Neil Jordan
Cast: Robert De Niro, Sean Penn, Demi Moore
Escaped cons are mistaken for priests as they desperately try to hightail it across the Canadian border. Filmed in Maple Ridge and Britannia Beach.

Who's Harry Crumb? (Comedy) 1989
Director: Paul Flaherty
Cast: John Candy, Jeffrey Jones, Annie Potts

Bumbling private eye Candy somehow manages to solve a kidnapping case. Vancouver stands in for Los Angeles.

1989

Bird on a Wire (Action/Comedy) 1989
Director: John Badham
Cast: Goldie Hawn, Mel Gibson, David Carradine
After Mel's cover in the Witness Protection Program gets blown, he and ex-girlfriend Goldie go on the lam. Filmed in Victoria as well as Vancouver.

Brothers in Arms (Horror) 1989
Director: George Jay Bloom III
Cast: Todd Allen, Jack Starrett
A young man fights against crazy backwoods folk who've made hunting people into a religion.

Cadence (Drama) 1989
Director: Martin Sheen
Cast: Martin Sheen, Charlie Sheen, Laurence Fishburne
An unruly soldier is placed in an all-black stockade and bonds with his brother prisoners by defying the local hard-ass sergeant. Shot near Kamloops, this film marked Sheen's directorial debut.

Deep Sleep (Drama) 1990
Director: Patricia Gruben
Cast: Megan Follows, Stuart Margolin, Patricia Collins
Art film about a troubled teen who tracks down the murky truth about her father's death.

Flesh Gordon Meets the Cosmic Cheerleaders (Cult) 1990
Director: Howard Ziehm
Cast: Vince Murdocco, Tony Travis, William Dennis Hunt, Robyn Kelly
An evil emperor threatens the universe with a bizarre impotence ray in this watered-down sequel to the soft-core spoof *Flesh Gordon.*

Friday the 13th Part 8: Jason Takes Manhattan (Horror) 1989
Director: Rob Hedden
Cast: Jensen Daggett, Scott Reeves, Peter Mark Richman
The only film in this teen horror series to be shot in Vancouver, part 8 finds the impossible-to-kill Jason taking a cruise to New York. While there he engages in his favourite hobby, killing.

The Grocer's Wife (Drama) 1991
Director: John Pozer
Cast: Simon Webb, Susinn McFarlen, Nicola Cavendish, Jay Brazeau
Stylish existential love story in which an introverted young man takes up with a stripper after his mother is hospitalized.

Narrow Margin (Action) 1990
Director: Peter Hyams
Cast: Gene Hackman, Anne Archer, James B. Sikking, M. Emmet Walsh
An L.A. cop tries to elude mobsters while protecting a murder witness on a train ride to Vancouver.

NeverEnding Story 2: The Next Chapter (Fantasy) 1990
Director: George Miller
Cast: Jonathan Brandis, Kenny Morrison, Clarissa Burt
Once again, a young boy is transported into the pages of a magical book to do battle against the forces of evil.

The Russia House (Drama) 1990
Director: Fred Schepisi
Cast: Sean Connery, Michelle Pfeiffer, Roy Scheider
A British publisher gets involved in espionage when a Russian woman sends him an unsolicited manuscript. Filmed partly on Bowen Island.

Short Time (Comedy) 1990
Director: Gregg Champion
Cast: Dabney Coleman, Matt Frewer, Teri Garr
After a Seattle cop is misdiagnosed with a terminal illness, he tries to get himself killed in the line of duty so his family will collect police benefits.

Terminal City Ricochet (Cult) 1990
Director: Zale Dalen
Cast: Mark Bennett, Peter Breck, Germain Houde, Jello Biafra
Zany B-movie satire about a newspaper delivery boy who inadvertently gets caught up in the political machinations of an evil mayoral candidate advocating self-help TV.

1990

Bingo (Comedy) 1991
Director: Matthew Robbins
Cast: Cindy Williams, David Rasche
Another take on the pooch-as-hero genre in which a dog chases his absent-minded master across the country and has all sorts of wacky adventures along the way.

Cafe Romeo (Romantic Comedy) 1991
Director: Rex Bromfield
Cast: Catherine Mary Stewart, Jonathan Crombie
Raised with Old World Italian traditions that no longer apply to them, six lifelong friends try to find their niche in the world outside their neighbourhood coffeeshop.

Chaindance (Drama) 1991
Director: Allan Goldstein
Cast: Michael Ironside, Brad Dourif, Rae Dawn Chong
A convict learns a lesson in life when chained to the wheelchair of a man with cerebral palsy.

Crooked Hearts (Drama) 1991
Director: Michael Bortman
Cast: Vincent D'Onofrio, Jennifer Jason Leigh, Peter Berg, Cindy Pickett, Juliette Lewis, Peter Coyote, Noah Wyle
Vancouver stands in for Tacoma, Washington, in this melodramatic story about a dysfunctional family's struggle to give one another "room to grow."

The Hitman (Action) 1991
Director: Aaron Norris
Cast: Chuck Norris, Michael Parks, Al Waxman, Alberta Watson
A police officer who is believed dead resurfaces as a hit man for a Seattle crime boss.

K2 (Adventure) 1992
Director: Franc Roddam
Cast: Michael Biehn, Matt Craven, Raymond J. Barry, Patricia Charbonneau
Adaptation of Patrick Meyer's stage play about a group of men who attempt to climb K2, the second highest and most treacherous mountain in the world. Filmed on location at Whistler-Blackcomb.

Kootenai Brown (Drama) 1991
Director: Allan Kroeker
Cast: Raymond Burr, Tom Burlinson, Donnelly Rhodes
The true tale of a man who marries a Métis woman and must kill to protect his family's survival. Shot in Barkerville.

Look Who's Talking Too (Comedy) 1990
Director: Amy Heckerling
Cast: John Travolta, Kirstie Alley, Olympia Dukakis
Baby Mikey (voice of Bruce Willis) gets some new playmates (voiced by Roseanne and Damon Wayans) while Kirstie Alley and John Travolta

reprise their roles as the helpless adults in this sequel to *Look Who's Talking*.

Mystery Date (Comedy) 1991
Director: Jonathan Wacks
Cast: Ethan Hawke, Terri Polo, Fisher Stevens
An insecure college student gets a date with the girl of his dreams, only to be mistaken for a crime figure and pursued by police, gangsters, and a strange florist.

Payoff (Action/Adventure) 1991
Director: Stuart Cooper
Cast: Keith Carradine, Kim Greist, Harry Dean Stanton
A man is haunted by the childhood memory of having unknowingly delivered a bomb that killed his parents.

The Pianist (Drama) 1991
Director: Claude Gagnon
Cast: Gail Travers, Macha Grenon, Eiji Okuda, Maury Chaykin
Coming-of-age story about two teenaged sisters and their passionate involvement with a world-famous pianist. Based on Ann Ireland's novel *A Certain Mr. Takahashi.*

The Resurrected (Horror) 1991
Director: Dan O'Bannon
Cast: John Terry, Jane Sibbet, Chris Sarandon
A man learns of a crazy ancestor who possessed the power to resurrect the dead. Based on H. P. Lovecraft's novel, *The Case of Charles Dexter Ward.*

Run (Action/Adventure) 1991
Director: Geoff Burrowes
Cast: Patrick Dempsey, Kelly Preston, Ken Pogue, Christopher Lawford
A young law student is wrongly accused of murdering the son of a mob boss and must now avoid both the vengeful father and the corrupt local police.

Silhouette (Suspense) 1990
Director: Lloyd Simandl
Cast: Marc Singer, Tracy Scoggins, Brion James
A public defender's obsessive desire to solve a murder leads her to a secret underground society.

Ski School (Comedy) 1990
Director: Damien Lee
Cast: Dean Cameron, Tom Breznahan, Patrick Laborteaux
This *Animal House*-inspired comedy about a school run by ski bums was filmed on and around Vancouver's local mountains.

XTRO 2 (Science Fiction) 1991
Director: Harry Davenport
Cast: Jan-Michael Vincent, Paul Koslo, Tara Buckman.
A scientist discovers a hideous creature hiding inside him after returning from a parallel universe.

1991

Airport In (Comedy)
Director: Erik Whittaker
Cast: Bill Evans
A cloak and dagger comedy set during a podiatrist's convention in Winnipeg.

Black Cat (Action) 1991
Director: Stephen Shin
Cast: Jade Leung, Simon Yam
After being programmed by the CIA, a young street-smart woman is turned into a professional killer.

Home Movie (Suspense) 1991
Director: Fred Frame
Cast: Ian Tracey, John Pyper-Ferguson
Fact and fiction blur as a group of friends act out a script about infidelity, lies, and trust.

Jennifer 8 (Suspense) 1992
Director: Bruce Robinson
Cast: Andy Garcia, Uma Thurman, John Malkovich, Lance Henriksen

A very wet Vancouver stands in for the coastal town of Eureka, California, where a burned-out L.A. cop finds himself on the trail of a serial killer.

Knight Moves (Mystery/Suspense) 1993
Director: Carl Schenkel
Cast: Christopher Lambert, Diane Lane, Tom Skerritt, Daniel Baldwin
An international chess tournament in the Pacific Northwest is the setting for this flick, where one of the top touring chess masters becomes the prime suspect in a macabre ritual murder.

Leaving Normal (Drama) 1992
Director: Edward Zwick
Cast: Christine Lahti, Meg Tilly, Lenny Von Dohlen, James Gammon
A tough, no-nonsense waitress and a naive young woman fleeing her abusive husband take a road trip from Normal, Wyoming, to Alaska. But their names aren't Thelma and Louise and this is quite a different story. Parts were filmed near Stewart and Squamish.

Never-Ending Summer (Drama) 1992
Director: Lawrence Cheng
Cast: Lawrence Cheng, DoDo Cheng
A Hong Kong yuppie immigrates to Vancouver where he falls for a devilish dragon lady.

North of Pittsburgh (Drama) 1989
Director: Richard Martin
Cast: Viveca Lindfors, Jeff Schultz, Byron Lucas
A small-time drug runner and his grandmother set out on an unlikely road trip.

Pure Luck (Comedy) 1991
Director: Nadia Tass
Cast: Martin Short, Danny Glover, Sheila Kelley, Scott Wilson, Harry Shearer
An Americanized version of Francis Veber's *Le Chevre*, featuring Danny Glover as a hapless detective who must work with a bumbling accountant and find the world's most accident-prone heiress.

Stay Tuned (Comedy) 1992
Director: Peter Hyams
Cast: John Ritter, Pam Dawber, Jeffrey Jones, Eugene Levy
A couch potato finds himself and his wife sucked into a TV world from hell after making a deal with the devil.

Time Runner (Science Fiction) 1992
Director: Michael Mazo
Cast: Mark Hamill, Rae Dawn Chong, Brion James
A time-travel adventure wherein the earth falls prey to a brutal alien attack. Also known as *In Exile*.

1992

Alive (Drama) 1993
Director: Frank Marshall
Cast: Ethan Hawke, Vincent Spano, Josh Hamilton
After a plane crashes in the Andes the survivors must do whatever they have to in order to stay alive. Filmed near Kootenay Mountain and adapted from Piers Paul Read's true story.

Black Cat 2 (Action) 1992
Director: Stephen Shin
Cast: Jade Leung
A young CIA agent travels to Russia to prevent the assassination of the premier by a bizarre nuclear-atomic agent.

The Burning Season (Drama) 1992
Director: Harvey Crossland
Cast: Ayub Khan Din, Akesh Gill, Om Puri

A young Indian woman flees her arranged marriage in North America to be with her lover in India.

The Crush (Suspense) 1993
Director: Alan Shapiro
Cast: Alicia Silverstone, Cary Elwes, Jennifer Rubin
Sexual thriller about a fourteen-year-old nymphet who becomes obsessed with the journalist who rents her parents' guest house.

Digger (Drama) 1994
Director: Robert Turner
Cast: Adam Hann-Byrd, Joshua Jackson, Barbara Williams, Timothy Bottoms, Olympia Dukakis, Leslie Nielsen
A young boy spends the summer with his grandparents on one of B.C.'s Gulf Islands and forms a friendship with a lad dying of leukemia. Shot near Brentwood Bay.

Harmony Cats (Comedy) 1993
Director: Sandy Wilson
Cast: Kim Coates
When an unemployed violinist hooks up with a travelling country and western band, he learns a little about life.

Impolite (Drama) 1992
Director: David Hauka
Cast: Suzy Joachim, Robert Wisden, Susan Hogan
A newspaper reporter runs into all kinds of trouble while tracking down a mystery man.

The Lotus Eaters (Comedy) 1993
Director: Paul Shapiro
Cast: Sheila McCarthy, R. H. Thomson
Family drama about a 1960s B.C. housewife whose husband falls for the hip new school teacher. Filmed on Galiano Island.

Needful Things (Horror) 1993
Director: Fraser Heston
Cast: Max von Sydow, Ed Harris, Bonnie Bedelia, Amanda Plummer, J. T. Walsh
A devilish old man opens a curiosity shop in a small Maine town. Filmed in Gibsons and based on the Stephen King novel.

The Portrait (Drama) 1993
Director: Arthur Penn
Cast: Gregory Peck, Lauren Bacall, Cecilia Peck
Sentimental story about an elderly couple facing the declining mental health of the husband, while their daughter attempts to finish their portrait.

Saviour of Souls 2 (Adventure) 1993
Director: David Lai
Cast: Andy Lau, Rosemond Kwan
A young man, obsessed with dreams of a woman "frozen in time," travels to the Arctic where his dreams come true.

Sleeping with Strangers (Comedy) 1994
Director: William T. Bolson
Cast: Adrienne Shelly, Neil Duncan, Sean Thompson
Two rival hotel owners get more than they bargained for when a drunken rock star and his actress girlfriend arrive in their small B.C. town. Filmed on location in Sooke.

Swallow in the Rain (Thriller) 1993
Director: David Lai
Two women, one a cop and one a drug addict, find themselves on the run in Vancouver after their boyfriends betray them. Also known as *Women on the Run*.

This Boy's Life (Drama) 1993
Director: Michael Caton-Jones
Cast: Robert De Niro, Ellen Barkin, Leonardo DiCaprio, Chris Cooper
The mother of a juvenile delinquent

moves to Seattle and tries to create a stable life for her son by marrying a "good provider." The new husband, however, decides to make the boy's life a living hell. Based on a true story.

Tomcat: Dangerous Desires (Horror) 1993
Director: Paul Donovan
Cast: Richard Grieco, Maryam D'Abo
As the result of a top-secret gene-splicing experiment, a young man takes on deadly feline attributes.

1993

The Air Up There (Comedy) 1994
Director: Paul Michael Glaser
Cast: Kevin Bacon, Charles Gitona Maina
An American basketball coach goes to Africa in hopes of recruiting the next Michael Jordan.

Another Stakeout (Action/Adventure) 1993
Director: John Badham
Cast: Richard Dreyfuss, Emilio Estevez, Rosie O'Donnell, Cathy Moriarty
This sequel to *Stakeout* sees the return of Dreyfuss and Estevez as a pair of inept police detectives. This time, they're joined in their crime-fighting antics by an assistant D.A. (O'Donnell) and her dog. Filmed on Bowen Island.

Arctic Blue (Adventure) 1994
Director: Peter Masterson
Cast: Rutger Hauer, Dylan Walsh, Rya Kihlstedt
A trapper suspected of murder shares some quality bonding time with a biologist while stuck in the Arctic. Parts were filmed near Britannia Beach.

Bad Company (Thriller) 1994
Director: Damian Harris
Cast: Ellen Barkin, Laurence Fishburne, Frank Langella
An ex-CIA operative tries to infiltrate an illicit company of former secret agents. Some lovely Vancouver sunset shots are welcome relief from the film's improbable plot.

Beyond Suspicion (Drama) 1994
Director: Paul Ziller
Cast: Jack Scalia, Stephanie Kramer
When a corrupt cop learns a photojournalist has succumbed to amnesia, he spares her life after she witnesses an illicit murder.

Breaking Point (Suspense) 1994
Director: Paul Ziller
Cast: Gary Busey, Darlanne Fluegel, Kim Cattrall
An ex-police officer comes out of retirement to catch the psycho who once almost killed him.

Bullet Proof Heart (Action/Adventure) 1994
Director: Mark Malone
Cast: Anthony LaPaglia, Mimi Rogers, Peter Boyle
A hit man is given a job he's not quite prepared for: kill a well-connected (and very attractive) woman who actually wants to die. Also known as *Killer*.

CrackerJack (Adventure) 1994
Director: Michael Mazo
Cast: Thomas Ian Griffith, Nastassia Kinski, Christopher Plummer
A renegade cop joins his brother's family in a getaway to the Rockies (played nicely, in parts, by Grouse Mountain) and happens upon a multimillion-dollar diamond heist.

Double Cross (Thriller) 1994
Director: Michael Keusch
Cast: Patrick Bergan, Jennifer Tilly, Kelly Preston

After having an affair with a beautiful blonde, a man must contend with blackmail and murder.

Edge of Deception (Drama) 1994
Director: George Mihalka
Cast: Mariel Hemingway, Stephen Shellen, Jennifer Rubin
A police lieutenant is pursued by a journalist doing a story on "cops who fall in love with killers."

Ernest Rides Again (Comedy) 1993
Director: John Cherry
Cast: Jim Varney
Infamous loon Ernest P. Worrell hijacks a henpecked history professor who believes England's *real* crown jewels are hidden inside a giant cannon.

Exquisite Tenderness (Horror) 1996
Director: Carl Schenkel
Cast: James Remar, Isabel Glasser
Riverview Hospital is the star in this bizarre medical horror tale about a surgeon and an intern who set out to discover the cause of various murders.

Far from Home: The Adventures of Yellow Dog (Adventure) 1994
Director: Phillip Borsos
Cast: Jesse Bradford, Bruce Davison, Mimi Rogers
After being lost at sea, a boy and his dog endure the elements on a small coastal island. Filmed near Lighthouse Park, this was director Phillip Borsos's last film.

Flinch (Suspense) 1994
Director: George Erschbamer
Cast: Judd Nelson, Nick Mancuso, Gina Gershon
A pair of models, working as department store mannequins, witness a murder.

Intersection (Drama) 1994
Director: Mark Rydell
Cast: Richard Gere, Sharon Stone, Lolita Davidovich, Martin Landau
Romantic triangle involving a wealthy architect, his frigid wife, and his lively mistress. Remake of the French film *Les Choses de la Vie.* In a rare star turn, Vancouver actually plays Vancouver.

Legends of the Fall (Drama) 1994
Director: Edward Zwick
Cast: Brad Pitt, Anthony Hopkins, Aidan Quinn, Julia Ormond
Sprawling family saga about three brothers raised in Montana by their father, a former cavalry officer who turned his back on bloodshed and the exploitation of Native people. Academy Award winner for best cinematography.

Look Who's Talking Now (Comedy) 1993
Director: Tom Ropelewski
Cast: John Travolta, Kirstie Alley, Olympia Dukakis
The third in the *Look Who's Talking* series. After taking the talking babies idea as far as they could, the filmmakers introduce us to a pair of talking dogs (voiced by Danny DeVito and Diane Keaton).

Max (Drama) 1993
Director: Charles Wilkinson
Cast: R. H. Thomson, Denise Crosby, Walter Dalton
When a yuppie couple's young son becomes ill, they pack up and move to the B.C. Interior where their expectations of living a more "natural" lifestyle are turned upside down.

The NeverEnding Story 3: Return to Fantasia (Fantasy) 1996
Director: Peter MacDonald
Cast: Jason James Richter, Melody Kay, Jack Black

Yet another chapter in the tale of a young boy who partakes of the adventures in a magical book. The film's computer-generated effects make up for its mediocre story.

The Raffle (Drama) 1994
Director: Gavin Wilding
Cast: Nicholas Lea, Bobby Dawson, Jennifer Clement, Jay Underwood, Mark Hamill
A couple of fellas travel the world in search of a woman who they think will make the perfect prize date.

Red Scorpion 2 (Action) 1994
Director: Michael Kennedy
Cast: Matt McColm, Michael Ironside, John Savage
A special agent leads a specially trained team up against a white supremacist group.

Starlight (Science Fiction) 1996
Director: Jonathan Kay
Cast: Willie Nelson, Rae Dawn Chong, Billy Wirth
An alien scientist travels to earth to bring back a man who can save her planet. Filmed in Nelson.

Timecop (Science Fiction) 1994
Director: Peter Hyams
Cast: Jean-Claude Van Damme, Mia Sara, Ron Silver, Gloria Reuben
In 2004, a new law enforcement agency polices time-travelling criminals and top officer Van Damme has to go back in time to try to catch their ringleader, an evil and ambitious senator. Based on the Dark Horse comic book series.

Tokyo Cowboy (Comedy) 1994
Director: Kathy Garneau
Cast: Christianne Hirt, Janne Mortil, Hiromoto Ida, Alec Willows
A Japanese man arrives in a small B.C. town (Merritt) to act out his wildest cowboy fantasies.

Whale Music (Drama) 1994
Director: Richard J. Lewis
Cast: Maury Chaykin, Cyndy Preston
Bizarre tale of an overweight, burned-out rock musician and the gorgeous runaway who takes over his life. Based on the novel by Paul Quarrington. Maury Chaykin earned a Genie Award for best actor.

White Fang 2: The Myth of the White Wolf (Adventure) 1994
Director: Ken Olin
Cast: Scott Bairstow, Charmaine Craig, Alfred Molina, Geoffrey Lewis
A young prospector and his pooch meet up with a Haida princess and become involved with her tribal village. Filmed near Britannia Beach.

Young Offenders (Drama) 1994
Director: Wong Lo Tak
Cast: Danny Wang, Emily Kwan, Jeremy Chin
A *Home Alone*-like story in which a wealthy young Taiwanese kid gets mixed up with a dangerous triad.

1994

Abducted 2: The Reunion (Thriller) 1994
Director: Boon Collins
Cast: Dan Haggerty, Jan-Michael Vincent, Donna Jason, Raquel Bianca, Debbie Rochon
In this unnecessary sequel to *Abducted*, a trio of girlfriends go camping and run into a crazed mountain man.

Andre (Comedy) 1994
Director: George Miller
Cast: Keith Carradine, Tina Majorino, Chelsea Field, Aidan Pendleton
A Maine family adopts a baby seal, who adopts them in return and refuses to leave. Based on a true story and filmed in Deep Cove.

Crash (Action) 1996
Director: Charles Wilkinson
Cast: Michael Biehn, Matt Craven
The sky's the limit when two men uncover an international money-laundering scheme.

Crying Freeman (Action) 1995
Director: Christophe Gans
Cast: Mark Dacascos, Julia Condra Douglas, Rae Dawn Chong
Based on a Japanese comic book about a hit man who cries after he makes his kills, this John Woo-inspired flick takes place in Vancouver.

Cyberteens in Love (Drama) 1995
Director: Brett Dowler
Cast: Martin Cummins, Justine Priestly, Hagen Beggs
A destitute young woman (played by Justine Priestly, Jason's younger sister) escapes from a Nazi-like orphanage to search for her family.

Dangerous Indiscretion (Suspense) 1994
Director: Richard Kletter
Cast: C. Thomas Howell, Malcolm McDowell
A young ad executive discovers that the woman he's seeing is married to a very powerful, and angry, man.

Deadly Sins (Drama) 1995
Director: Michael Robinson
Cast: Alyssa Milano, David Keith
A cop and a nun try to solve the mysterious murders of young teen girls at a private Catholic school.

Devotion (Drama)
Director: Mindy Kaplan
Cast: Jan Derbyshire, Kate Twa, Steve Adams
A bizarre love triangle threatens to disrupt the lives of its participants, three women.

Double Happiness (Comedy/Drama) 1995
Director: Mina Shum
Cast: Sandra Oh, Allanah Ong, Callum Rennie, Stephen Cheng, Francis You
Vancouver director Mina Shum's charming story about a twentysomething Chinese-Canadian woman trying to find her way in the world while still attempting to adhere to her parents' strict rules and traditions. Sandra Oh earned a Genie Award for best actress.

Dream Man (Comedy/Drama)
Director: Rene Bonniere
Cast: Bruce Greenwood, Andrew McCarthy, Patsy Kensit
Working in his home town of Vancouver, Greenwood plays a plainclothes detective whose partner, an ex-lover with ESP, compromises their case when she has an affair with a suspect.

Fear (Thriller) 1996
Director: James Foley
Cast: "Marky" Mark Wahlberg, Reese Witherspoon, William Petersen, Amy Brenneman
The "psycho-boyfriend" genre attempts a comeback in this odd film about a father who tries to protect his teenaged daughter from an obsessive admirer. Shot partly in Howe Sound.

Gold Diggers: The Legend of Bear Mountain (Family Adventure) 1995
Director: Ted Bessell
Cast: Anna Chlumsky, Christina Ricci
A pair of teenaged girls go hunting for gold and discover a few life lessons along the way. Filmed in part near Deep Cove and in the Fraser Valley.

Hard Evidence (Thriller) 1995
Director: Michael Kennedy
Cast: Gregory Harrison, Joan Severance, Cali Timmins

A real-estate developer tries to clear his name after his mistress is found dead.

Hideaway (Science Fiction/Thriller) 1994
Director: Brett Leonard
Cast: Jeff Goldblum, Christine Lahti, Alicia Silverstone, Jeremy Sisto
Revived after a fatal car crash, Goldblum finds himself psychically connected to a killer. Based on the novel by Dean R. Koontz. The Lower Mainland doubles as Washington State.

Highway of Heartache (Cult) 1994
Director: Gregory Wild
Cast: Barbara Chamberlin, Pat Patterson, The Big Wigs
A campy and controversial musical tale about a country and western singer's tragic life on the road.

The Hunted (Action) 1994
Director: Jonathan Lawton
Cast: Christopher Lambert, John Lone, Joan Chen
While visiting Japan, an American businessman witnesses a murder and finds himself on the run from a modern-day Ninja clan.

Kissed (Drama) 1996
Director: Lynne Stopkewich
Cast: Molly Parker, Peter Outerbridge, Jay Brazeau, Natasha Morley
A girl-next-door recounts the events leading up to her discovery of the hidden life of the dead.

Little Panda (Adventure) 1995
Director: Chris Cain
Cast: Ryan Slater, Isabella Hoffman
Chinese adventure about that most cherished of animals—the panda.

Little Women (Drama) 1994
Director: Gillian Armstrong
Cast: Winona Ryder, Susan Sarandon, Gabriel Byrne, Trini Alvarado, Samantha Mathis, Kirsten Dunst, Mar Andersons
The fourth screen adaptation of the Louisa May Alcott novel about four devoted sisters who eventually have to leave their New England home and start their own lives. Ryder earned an Academy Award nomination for her performance as Jo. Oscar nominations were also earned for costume design and score. Filmed in part on Vancouver Island.

Magic in the Water (Family Adventure) 1995
Director: Rick Stevenson
Cast: Mark Harmon, Harley Jane Kozack, Joshua Jackson
Heartwarming adventure about a couple of kids who discover a sea monster living in their local lake. Filmed in Kaslo. Winner of the Genie Award for best cinematography.

Malicious (Thriller) 1996
Director: Ian Corson
Cast: Molly Ringwald, Patrick McGaw
After seducing a young man, a psychotic woman becomes obsessed with him.

Man of the House (Comedy) 1995
Director: James Orr
Cast: Chevy Chase, Farrah Fawcett, Jonathan Taylor Thomas
After a boy schemes to get rid of his mother's new love interest, he learns the guy is not so bad after all. Vancouver again stands in for Seattle.

Midnight Heat (Thriller) 1995
Director: Harvey Frost
Cast: Tim Matheson, Mimi Craven
A football player is framed for the murder of his lover's husband.

Power of Attorney (Drama) 1995
Director: Howard Himelstein
Cast: Danny Aiello, Elias Koteas, Rae Dawn Chong
A young lawyer is hoodwinked into defending a member of the mob.

The Road Home (Drama) 1996
Director: Dean Hamilton
Cast: Charles Martin Smith, Danny Aiello, Kris Kristofferson, Mickey Rooney
Rooney plays Father Flanagan in this family adventure based on the 1938 classic *Boys Town*, in which he starred as a child.

Rumble in the Bronx (Action) 1996
Director: Stanley Tong
Cast: Jackie Chan, Anita Mui
While visiting the U.S. for a wedding, a Hong Kong cop wreaks havoc on American hoodlums and mobsters. Vancouver laughably tries to double as the Bronx.

The Scarlet Letter (Drama) 1995
Director: Roland Joffe
Cast: Demi Moore, Gary Oldman, Robert Duvall
Another remake of Nathaniel Hawthorne's classic book in which the disgraced preacher *doesn't* die, but instead rides off into the sunset. Filmed in part near Campbell River.

Ski School 2 (Comedy)
Director: David Mitchell
Cast: Dean Cameron, Heather Campbell
Predictable sequel to the *Animal House*-inspired film about a school run by ski bums.

Someone to Die for (Drama) 1995
Director: Clay Boris
Cast: Corbin Bernsen, Rob Stewart, Ally Walker
A sexy crime reporter vies for the affection of a police detective after his daughter is murdered.

Suspicious Agenda (Drama) 1995
Director: Clay Borris
Cast: Richard Grieco, Nick Mancuso, Jim Byrnes
A pair of cops investigate a string of murders which they are believed to be responsible for.

Virtual Assassins (Science Fiction) 1995
Director: Robert Lee
Cast: Michael Dudikoff, Brion James, Suki Kaiser
A crazed villain pits a deadly computer virus against the world. Dudikoff stars as the hapless hero who saves the day.

Wings of Courage (Adventure/Drama) 1996
Director: Jean-Jacques Annaud
Cast: Craig Sheffer, Tom Hulce, Elizabeth McGovern, Val Kilmer
This first feature-length IMAX film tells the story of a courageous young pilot. B.C.'s Rocky Mountains (doubling as the Andes) are breathtaking.

1995

Ace Ventura 2: When Nature Calls (Comedy) 1995
Director: Don Thorin
Cast: Jim Carrey
Sequel to the wild *Ace Ventura: Pet Detective*. This time out Carrey hams it up in Africa. The film's opening sequence was shot near the Panorama Ridge in the B.C. Interior.

Alaska (Action/Adventure) 1996
Director: Fraser Heston
Cast: Thora Birch, Vincent Kartheiser, Dirk Benedict, Charlton Heston
A family picture about a pair of siblings who brave the Alaskan wilderness to rescue their bush-pilot father after his plane has crashed. Filmed in Whistler.

Big Bully (Comedy) 1996
Director: Steve Miner
Cast: Rick Moranis, Tom Arnold, Don Knotts
A successful writer returns home to teach and discovers that his child-

hood nemesis is now the shop teacher at their old high school.

Bliss (Romance/Drama) 1996
Director: Lance Young
Cast: Craig Sheffer, Sheryl Lee, Terence Stamp
A young married man discovers unexpected truths about his wife after she starts seeing an unconventional sex therapist.

Bounty Hunters (Action)
Director: George Erschbamer
Cast: Michael Dudikoff, Lisa Howard
A pair of rival bounty hunters team up to bring down a bail jumper.

Carpool (Comedy) 1996
Director: Arthur Hiller
Cast: Tom Arnold, David Paymer, Rhea Perlman, Rod Steiger
A convenience store robber holds a stressed-out businessman hostage—along with his five-kid carpool.

The Ex (Thriller) 1996
Director: Mark Lester
Cast: Yancy Butler, Nick Mancuso
A man struggles to keep his estranged wife from destroying his new family.

Final Cut (Suspense) 1996
Director: Roger Christian
Cast: Sam Elliott, Anne Ramsey, Charles Martin Smith
A bomb expert is pitted against a madman terrorizing a city that is supposed to be Seattle, but which looks suspiciously like Vancouver.

For a Few Lousy Dollars (Comedy) 1996
Director: Stephen Benoit
Cast: Ian Tracey, Ben Ratner, Frank Cassini
A couple of generation Xers' fight over the pros and cons of robbing a mob-run pizzeria.

Happy Gilmore (Comedy) 1996
Director: Dennis Dugan
Cast: Adam Sandler, Carl Weathers, Julie Bowen, Frances Bay, Bob Barker
A would-be hockey player decides to take out his frustrations on the golf course when his grandmother's house is confiscated by the IRS. Just about every golf course in the Lower Mainland participated in this film.

Hard Core Logo (Drama) 1996
Director: Bruce McDonald
Cast: Hugh Dillon, Bernie Coulson, Callum Rennie
The saga of a fictional punk band's rise to fame. Based on the book by Michael Turner.

Homeward Bound 2: Lost in San Francisco (Family/Adventure) 1996
Director: David Ellis
Cast: Robert Hayes, Kim Griest, Kevin Chevalia
Household pets triumph over adversity when they're left behind in the big city. That city is Vancouver, this time posing as San Francisco.

Jumanji (Fantasy/Adventure) 1995
Director: Joe Johnston
Cast: Robin Williams, Bonnie Hunt, Kirsten Dunst, David Alan Grier
Williams is in his element when a magical board game comes to life and wreaks havoc on its players and their small town. The Lower Mainland doubles nicely as the New Hampshire hamlet where computer-generated pachyderms run amok.

Live Bait (Drama) 1995
Director: Bruce Sweeney
Cast: Tom Scholte, Babz Chula, Micki Maunsell
An older woman becomes involved with a younger man in this May-December romantic drama.

Man with a Gun (Drama) 1995
Director: David Wyles
Cast: Michael Madsen, Jennifer Tilly, Gary Busey
A hit man must decide whether or not to knock off his beautiful girlfriend, or her innocent twin sister instead. Based on Hugh C. Rae's *The Shroud Society.*

Mask of Death (Suspense) 1996
Director: David Mitchell
Cast: Lorenzo Lamas, Billy Dee Williams, Rae Dawn Chong
After a police officer's wife is murdered, he assumes the killer's identity and goes under cover to seek justice.

One Foot in Heaven (Drama) 1995
Director: Brian Barnard
Cast: Malcolm Alexander, Jody Andrews, Janet Craig
A heart-warming tale about five seniors who escape from an old folks' home and travel from Dawson Creek to Vancouver.

Once in a Blue Moon (Drama) 1995
Director: Phillip Spink
Cast: Cody Serpa, Simon Baker, Cheryl Wilson, Mike MacDonald
The whimsical story of two young boys who live in a fantasy world and their plot to exact revenge on the local bullies. Set in 1967 during Canada's centennial.

Past Perfect (Science Fiction/Thriller) 1996
Director: Jonathan Heap
Cast: Eric Roberts, Nick Mancuso, Saul Rubinek
A cop encounters time-travelling executioners who are wiping out future killers.

Profile for Murder (Thriller) 1995
Director: David Winning
Cast: Lance Henriksen, Jeff Wincott
A psychologist is attracted to a notorious businessman who has been arrested for the vicious slayings of several young women.

Ski Nuts (Comedy) 1996
Director: David Mitchell
Cast: Keith Coogan, Stacey Keanan, Lochlyn Munro
Another silly hijinks-on-the-slopes flick wherein the heroes must unite and triumph over adversity.

Stiff (Comedy/Thriller) 1996
Director: Mark Sawers
Cast: Taylor Nichols, Laura Harris
A successful author gets a case of writer's block and takes refuge in a seaside cabin. Shot near Qualicum Beach.

Suzie Q (Comedy) 1996
Director: John Richard Blizek
Cast: Justin Whalin, Amy Jo Johnson, Shelley Long
The ghost of a young girl enlists the help of a boy to discover why her parents lost their home to the bank.

Tales from the Crypt: Bordello of Blood (Horror) 1996
Director: Gilbert Adler
Cast: Dennis Miller, Erika Eleniak, Chris Sarandon, Corey Feldman
A private detective gets pulled into a strange world of hookers and vampires. Vancouver's back streets and alleys never looked better.

Underworld (Thriller) 1996
Director: Roger Christian
Cast: Denis Leary, Joe Mantegna, Annabella Sciorra
A film noir flick about an ex-con gangster who plots a way to avenge the death of his father.

Unforgettable (Thriller) 1996
Director: John Dahl
Cast: Ray Liotta, Linda Fiorentino
After his wife is murdered, pathologist Liotta takes on the memories of

several dead people in order to solve the crime. Vancouver stands in once again for . . . Seattle.

Urban Safari (Comedy) 1996
Director: Reto Salimbini
Cast: David Naughton, Linda Kash, Donnelly Rhodes
A couple fake a vacation and end up hiding out in their apartment.

1996

Bad Moon (Thriller)
Director: Eric Red
Cast: Mariel Hemingway, Michael Pare, Mason Gamble
This intense thriller pits a single mom, her son, and a dog named Thor against the boy's evil uncle.

Bounty Hunters 2 (Action)
Director: George Erschbamer
Cast: Michael Dudikoff, Lisa Howard
A sequel to *Bounty Hunters*, Dudikoff and Howard again play a pair of rival bounty hunters who team up to bring down the bad guys.

Death Game (Action)
Director: Randolph Cheveldave
Cast: Timothy Bottoms, David McCallum
In a futuristic world (Vancouver doubling as L.A.) ravaged by chaos, a down-on-his-luck cop is hired to find a wealthy man's missing daughter.

Deep Rising (Adventure)
Director: Steve Sommers
Cast: Treat Williams, Kevin J. O'Connor
In the tradition of classic 1950s sea monster movies and 1970s disaster movies, a luxury cruise liner indeed courts disaster when it is attacked by a giant sea monster.

Exception to the Rule (Suspense)
Director: David Winning
Cast: Sean Young, William Devane, Kim Cattrall
A diamond-trader's pregnant wife becomes embroiled in a sordid affair that turns out to be a scam to steal precious gems.

Excess Baggage (Adventure)
Director: Marci Brambilla
Cast: Alicia Silverstone, Christopher Walken, Benecio del Toro, Nicholas Turturro, Harry Connick, Jr.
When a bored and neglected rich girl tries to get the attention of her father, she ends up staging her own kidnapping. Vancouver and Victoria stand in for the Pacific Northwest.

Firestorm (Action)
Director: Dean Semler
Cast: Howie Long
Set in the wilds of Yellowstone National Park, a group of convicts take a hostage, burn down a forest, and try to escape—not necessarily in that order.

Free Willy 3 (Family/Adventure)
Director: Sam Pillsbury
Cast: Jason James Richter, August Schellenberg
A teenager befriends a young boy whose father likes to kill whales. This time Willy the whale is saved from illegal poachers.

horsey (Drama)
Director: Kirsten Clarkson
Cast: Holly Ferguson, Todd Kerns, Ryan Robbins, Victoria Deschanel
Director Clarkson's semi-autobiographical story about a struggle against heroin addiction.

The Prisoner of Zenda Inc. (Drama/Adventure)
Director: Stefan Scaini
Cast: William Shatner, Jonathan Jackson, Richard Jackson
A modern-day corporate spin is put on this fifth film adaptation of Anthony Hope's swashbuckling tale about two identical men who switch places.

The Process (Action)
Director: Ernie Reyes, Jr.
Cast: Ernie Reyes, Jr., Corin Nemec
Vancouver is the site of an international martial arts competition during which one of its competitors gets lost in the city's urban jungle.

The Sixth Man (Comedy)
Director: Randall Miller
Cast: Marlon Wayans, Kadeem Hardison
The ghost of a Washington state basketball player hits the court (GM Place) in order to help his losing teammates.

Smart Alec (Action/Suspense)
Director: Roger Christian
Cast: Patrick Stewart
Computer technology and special effects play big roles in this *Die Hard*-like yarn about a boy who keeps one step ahead of the terrorists who have taken over his school.

Warriors of Virtue (Action/Fantasy)
Director: Ronnie Yu
Cast: Mario Yedidia, Michael Dubrow
In the magical land of Tao, a young boy finds the secret of inner strength when he experiences the true meaning of the five virtues.

Wounded (Action)
Director: Richard Martin
Cast: Madchen Amick, Adrian Pasdar, Graham Greene
A pair of conservation officers bite off more than they can chew when tracking down a nasty bear poacher.

PLACES INDEX

PEOPLE INDEX

FILM AND TELEVISION INDEX

SELECTED BIBLIOGRAPHY

Books

Browne, Colin. *Motion Picture Production in B.C. 1898–1940*. Victoria: British Columbia Provincial Archives, 1979.

Duffy, Dennis J. *Camera West: B.C. on Film 1941–1965*. Victoria: Provincial Archives of B.C., 1986.

Film Canadiana 1969–1984. Ottawa: Canadian Film Institute, 1969.

LuKanic, Steven A. *Film Actor's Guide*. Los Angeles: Lone Eagle Publishing Co., 1995.

Marill, Alvin H. *Movies Made for Television: The Telefeature and the Miniseries 1964–1984*. New York: New York Zoetrope, 1984.

Milne, Tom. *VideoHound's Golden Movie Retriever 1996*. Detroit: Visible Ink Press, 1996.

Morris, Peter. *The Film Companion*. Richmond Hill, Ontario: Festival of Festivals/Irwin Publishing, 1984.

Nash, Jay Robert and Stanley Ralph Ross. *Motion Picture Guide 1927–1983*. Chicago: Cinebooks Inc., 1985.

PERIODICALS

Focal Point. 1993–95. B.C. Film Commission, Vancouver, B.C.

The Hollywood Reporter. 1987–91,1995. B.C. Special Report Editions.

The New York Times Film Reviews. 1914–68. *New York Times.*

Reel West Magazine. 1985–95, Reel West Productions Inc., Burnaby, B.C.

REPORTS

Burgess, Bob. *Location Filming in the GVRD*. Vancouver: Greater Vancouver Regional District, 1987.

ACKNOWLEDGEMENTS

Thanks to the following for their help on this project: Grandee Englehart, Trevor Hodgson, Justin Caulder, Graham Peate, Sylvia Bartell, Hugh Pickett, Bonnie Morishita, Chris DeVito, Len Wong, Kyle Kirkwood, Neil Bliss, Frank Garcia, Sal Nensi, Glen Winter, Christine Mark, James Bamford, Mar Andersons, Mark Hope, Jaime Bridle, Ward Bond, Stefan Fernitich, Phil Sanderson, the Rosenfelds and Tom Crowe. Thanks also go to the B.C. Film Commission, B.C. Film, C & C Communications, ETC Concepts, Ron Harvey, the local film community, and the rest of my family, friends, and associates who are too numerous to mention. A final thank you to the sites and organizations listed within these pages for co-operating, most of the time.

ABOUT THE AUTHOR

Ken MacIntyre has been involved in Vancouver's arts and entertainment industry for ten years. He has written for *B.C. Film News, Role Call Publications, Comics Scene Magazine,* and CITR UBC Radio. He has worked as a production assistant on the series *Madison,* and as a marketing representative for Paramount Pictures Canada.